Knowing

BRITISH HISTORY TOPICS

A History of

The Mass Media

Olivia Bennett

Bell & Hyman

Acknowledgements

The author and publishers would like to thank the following for permission to reproduce photographs, illustrations or extracts from books, newspapers and magazines. In particular, we would like to acknowledge the material taken from Susan Briggs' *Those Radio Times* published by Weidenfeld and Nicolson.

Associated Newspapers Group PLC 13(T), 14, 15(T & BR), 17, 25(B), 40, 42(M)   Associated Press 5(TR), 41(B)   BBC Hulton Picture Library 7, 11, 26, 27, 34   *BBC Handbook 1937*, BBC Publications, **(extract) 35**   Bell, Lady Florence, *At the Works: Study of a Manufacturing Town, Middlesborough*, Virago Press, **(extract) 18**   Briggs, S., *Those Radio Times*, Weidenfeld and Nicolson Ltd **(extracts) 23, 24, 29**   British Film Institute 31, 32, 33   British Newspaper Library 9   Cadbury Group of Companies 12, 36   Camera Press 45(T), 47(T)   Channel Four Television 38   Chapman, C., *Russell of The Times*, Unwin Hyman Ltd, **(extracts) 10**   Chiltern Radio 29(L)   City of Birmingham, City Museums and Art Gallery ("The Travelling Companions") 19(L)   Clayre, Alisdair, *Nature and Industrialisation: An Anthology*, Oxford University Press **(extract) 24**   Fenwick Miller, F., *Biography of Harriet Martineau*, (*Eminent Women* series, ed. J. H. Ingram), W. H. Allen, **(extract) 22**   Granada Television 37(L)   *The Guardian* 14   *Hansard 1953*, H.M.S.O. Publications, **(extract) 47**   Illustrated London News Picture Library 8   Independent Broadcasting Authority (Library), **(extracts) 37**   *Mandy* (D C Thomson & Co Ltd) 21(T)   The Mansell Collection 4, 5(TL), 6, 16(B), 18, 20, 30   Martineau, Harriet, *Autobiography*, Virago Press **(extract) 30**   Mary Evans Picture Library 10, 19(R), 22   Jo Nesbitt (*Images of Women*) 21(B)   *The Observer* **(extract) 17**   42(R)   Photosource 25(T)   Popperfoto 42(L)   Punch 23   *The Radio Times*, BBC Publications, **(extracts) 23, 26, 29, 33, 46**   Radio Times 23   (Radio Times/Pye) 24, 33   35(L), 46   Rex Features 44   Sally and Richard Greenhill 28, 35(R), 47(B)   *The Sunday Times* 16(T)   *The Sunday Times*, article by Peter Wilby, **(extract) 41**   Syndication International (1986) Ltd; (IPC), 21(T)   *The Times* 9, 15(B)   Topham Picture Library 46   UNESCO 29(L)   Weekly Dispatch (British Newspaper Library) 13(B)   Wendy Wallace 45(B)

Published in 1987 by
BELL & HYMAN
An imprint of Unwin Hyman Limited
Denmark House
37–39 Queen Elizabeth Street
London SE1 2QB

British Library Cataloguing in Publication Data
Bennett, Olivia
A history of the mass media. —(Knowing British history topics)
1. Mass media—History
I. Title. II. Series
302.2'34'09   P90

ISBN 0–7135–2624–6

Typeset in Great Britain by
Latimer Trend & Company Ltd, Plymouth

Printed and bound by
BAS Printers Limited, Over Wallop, Hampshire

Contents

Words printed in italics are explained in the Glossary.

To the Teacher

This book follows the same format as other titles in the series Knowing British History Topics. It caters for mixed ability classes and some questions, for example those involving a survey, can be done at the simplest level or expanded into a more complex project. Where appropriate, children are encouraged to draw upon their own experience and to use their imagination. There is plenty of scope to develop more ambitious project work. An obvious example is for the class to produce their own newspaper. A particularly useful aspect for them to explore first-hand is the process of selective editing: how to choose the items to include and deciding on their relative importance. There are also opportunities for project work involving the use of tape and video recorders (making their own radio programme, conducting a survey or series of interviews, recording a discussion about or a dramatic reconstruction of some of the incidents and issues described, etc) which will give pupils some practical experience of the problems and questions involved.

Personal experience of the mass media is an aspect which can also be explored further, again using communication technology in the process. Since virtually everyone's life in Britain is touched by the media to a greater or lesser degree, pupils could interview a variety of people to build up a historical picture of the impact of the mass media on their local community over, say, the last 70 years. This and other projects (eg the history of the local paper) invite display work, or the information could be presented in the form of a book, or recorded on audio or video cassette.

A historical approach to the subject of the mass media is rare but the popularity of Media Studies means there is plenty of complementary further reading which explores the impact of mass media on contemporary life.

Chapter 1　The Global Village

Have you ever heard someone describe today's world as a 'global village'? In a village, everyone hears about events—and is affected by them—very quickly. Today, news travels so fast that we soon know what's going on, even on the other side of the globe. We hear about an earthquake in Mexico, for example, just hours after it strikes. We watch the rescue efforts almost as they happen. We see television pictures, in our own sitting rooms, of the suffering caused by war and famine thousands of miles away. Improved global communications have made the whole world like a small village.

Most of our information about world events comes to us via the mass communications media. The mass media are the means through which the mass of people receive not only news and information but also entertainment. Television is a mass medium. So are radio, films, newspapers, books and magazines. Their *function* is communication: they inform, educate and entertain us.

A town crier, who walked through the streets and called out the news.

1.　**What is a mass medium? Give three examples of mass media.**

2.　**What is the function of the mass media?**

News for the few

In the last century, most people knew little about events which took place outside the places where they lived or worked. News of the wider world took a long time to reach them. In 1805, for example, it took more than two weeks for the news of Britain's victory at Trafalgar to reach the front page of *The Times*. Information, and therefore discussion, about important events and issues was usually only for the rich and powerful. In other words, the communications media were not mass media—they informed only the educated few.

Even at the beginning of this century, there were no radios, televisions or record players. People made their own entertainment and the street was the centre of social life for most working people. There were travelling street musicians and entertainers, but although they carried gossip and news from one town to the next, they were not a reliable source of information. The only mass medium in existence was print, and news-papers were expensive, so only the rich bought them regularly.

This is how one woman described the way her village received news when she was young, about 60 years ago:

'I lived in a small Somerset village. Towards the end of the 1920s and in the early 1930s, radio became part of our lives. Before this, we never thought of hearing news regularly. News came to us after days, even weeks. The local squire, doctor or vicar might have a national Sunday paper, which would be passed around the village. Otherwise, we saw mainly local papers, once or twice a week. On special occasions, such as the King's Birthday, Budget Day or some important foreign event, there would be a public reading of the papers in the Parish Hall.'

(Beatrice Kington, born 1914)

3.　**Which mass medium changed the way that people in the village were informed about world events?**

4.　**How many times a day does your family hear the news? How does this compare with how often the news came to the Somerset village before the arrival of radio?**

5.　**Why do you think only the local squire, doctor or vicar would have bought a national paper?**

A travelling street musician in London, 1895. Street entertainers and traders brought news and gossip from one neighbourhood to the next.

So perhaps another way of looking at the 'global village', rather than that the world has shrunk to a village, is that most people's horizons have stretched. They are now educated and entertained by news of people, places and events from all around the globe.

Mass communication today

Most people in Britain use the mass media several times a day. Three out of four people read a national morning newspaper every day. Every week, people watch television for an average of 21 hours—almost a whole day! Practically every home has at least one radio.

6. **Make a chart like the one below and fill it in for yourself over one week. Put in the number of times that you watch television/listen to the radio/go to the cinema/read a book, magazine or newspaper. If possible, keep a note of the amount of time that you spend doing each thing, too.**

MON						
TUES						
WED						
THURS						
FRI						
SAT						
SUN						
TOTAL						

Today news travels fast. Sometimes we see news being made. In 1986 many people watching the launch of the American space shuttle on television saw it explode in mid-air.

Compare your chart with those of others in your group. Find a way of clearly displaying the information that you have gathered, perhaps by using a bar chart or pie chart.

The mass media have given us much greater opportunities for entertainment and education. They have also altered some of the traditional ways in which we work and relax. One major change, brought about by television, is that most entertainment now takes place in the home, instead of in the street, music hall or social club.

Some people are concerned about these changes. One particular fear about the mass media is that they have a great potential to influence people. They make it possible for one person to put across ideas and opinions to literally millions of others. This is why the relationship between the media and people in positions of power has always been an important—and sometimes worrying—issue.

7. **We receive most of our information about the world through the media. Do you think that it is important that the media should be free to report the news without government control? If so, why?**

Chapter 2   The First Newspapers

Before the invention of printing, information travelled largely by word of mouth. Few people could read or write. Town criers called out news and public announcements. Sometimes, *bulletins* of important news were put up in public places. In 1455, Johann Gutenberg invented movable type. For the first time, fast and cheap printing became possible. Using presses like the one in the picture, news, stories and teachings could be passed on to large numbers of people. More people learnt to read, although by and large education was still available only to the rich and those in the Church. There was a great increase in the number of inventions and in learning as people read about new ideas, discussed and improved upon them. They then wrote about their views and passed them on to others.

The first printing was done by carving words on to a wooden block. This was covered in ink and pressed hard on to paper. Gutenberg invented movable, separate pieces of type for each letter. They could be rearranged into different words and used many times.

1. **How did the invention of printing help to spread ideas and knowledge to many more people?**

After Gutenberg's invention, the printed word began to appear all over Europe. There were no regular news bulletins but leaflets were distributed whenever there was really important news. By the sixteenth century, some very wealthy men had started keeping a personal newswriter to keep them informed about events abroad.

2. **Why might a wealthy merchant in England want to know about events in other countries?**

Pamphlets

Pamphleteering began in the sixteenth century. People who felt strongly about a particular political, social or religious matter wrote about it in a short *pamphlet*. Each pamphleteer expressed his point of view and tried to persuade his readers to agree with him. Reading and writing pamphlets became a popular way of carrying on *debates* among educated people. In particular, fierce arguments were conducted by pamphleteers during England's Civil War. Pamphlets remained a popular means of communication until the last century.

3. **The pamphlets and newsheets of the sixteenth century were the 'parents' of the** modern newspaper. An important part of any paper today is the 'leader'. This is an article that expresses an opinion on an important issue. It is usually written by the editor. In what way is his or her purpose similar to that of a pamphleteer?

By the early 1600s, newsletters had begun to appear on a regular basis in Britain, not just on special occasions. They were called 'corantes'. The name comes from the French word 'courir', meaning 'to run', and they were so called because they had to be delivered round the country very quickly. In 1641, a newsletter called *Diurnal Occurrences* was started ('Diurnal' means 'of the day' or 'daily'). As well as general news, it reported events in Parliament.

4. **Find out what was happening in the 1640s in England. Explain in a few sentences why people might have been anxious to have news of events in Parliament at this time.**

Each issue of *Diurnal Occurrences* and the other 'corantes' was read by lots of people, who met together in inns, clubs and coffee houses to discuss the news and the latest pamphlets. Coffee houses provided free copies in order to attract customers. Eventually, the government became anxious about the content of the newsletters,

Coffee house (1714). Reading the news was a sociable activity. There was much fierce discussion and debate!

The Daily Courant, *11 March, 1702. It cost a penny (80p in modern money).*

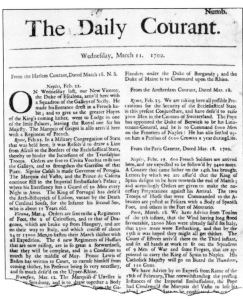

which they thought might be critical of them. In 1660 they passed laws that stopped all papers except the *London Gazette*, which they printed themselves.

The ban was lifted in 1695. Soon, several new papers were being published. England's first paper to be printed every day was *The Daily Courant*. It cost one penny. In 1702, when the paper was founded, this was not cheap. A single copy would be read by about ten people, each hiring the paper for a small fee.

News for the rich

Knowledge and discussion of current affairs was still largely confined to the rich and educated. Not only were papers expensive but most people could not read. The news was read aloud to crowds in market towns but country people had to wait weeks for important news to reach them.

Some members of the government were still suspicious of newspapers. They would have preferred most people to remain ignorant of what really went on in the world. So, instead of banning papers again—an unpopular move—they introduced a tax to keep them out of the reach of anyone but the rich. A Stamp Tax of one penny per sheet of newspaper began in 1712. This 'tax on knowledge', as its critics called it, continued for more than a hundred years.

---

5. Why do you think critics of the Stamp Tax called it a 'tax on knowledge'?

---

6. The government recently considered putting a tax called VAT on books and newspapers. Why do you think that many people opposed this?

---

7. Copy out this crossword and complete it. You will need to draw a grid 12 squares across and 12 squares high. The number of letters in the answer is given (in brackets) at the end of each clue.

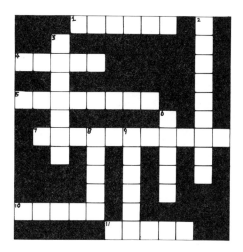

Across
1. The person who controls the content of a newspaper, and usually writes 9 Down. (6)
4. Before the invention of printing, the town ----- called out the news in market towns. (5)
5. The name given to the first regular newsletters. (8)
7. The name given to a person who wrote pamphlets. (11)
10. The ------- *Courant* was the first paper to be printed every day. (5)

11. The first mass communication medium. (5)
Down
2. Johann -------- invented movable type. (9)
3. Another word for 'daily'. (7)
6. The ----- Tax was also called 'a tax on knowledge'. (5)
8. The first daily newspaper cost one -----. (5)
9. An article in a newspaper that expresses opinion about an important matter. (6)

Chapter 3 Freedom of the Press

The government's Stamp Tax meant that few people could afford a regular newspaper. Papers lost money. Some closed down. Others often took money (*bribes*) from government servants, businessmen and others in order to survive. In return, they printed stories the way these people wanted them told. The idea that the Press should be free from such attempts to control what it printed was not yet accepted. The history of the newspaper industry tells us about the first battles for the freedom of the Press. Their outcome was important for all mass media.

---

1. **Why did the Stamp Tax prevent many people from reading newspapers?**

2. **The Stamp Tax meant that fewer newspapers were sold. How did their publishers make up the money they lost?**

3. **How did the need to accept bribes affect the newspapers' freedom to report the news?**

In 1729, the government made another difficulty for newspapers. They banned their right to report Parliamentary debates. Journalists tried all sorts of ways to get around this. They would send someone with an excellent memory to listen to the speeches. Afterwards, he would write down everything he could remember. The writer Samuel Johnson was very good at writing up debates. He wrote speeches that were so much better than anything the real MPs might have said that often they did not want to deny them!

One MP, John Wilkes, thought the ban was wrong. He fought hard to protect journalists and newspaper publishers from government action against them. He made many enemies in the government but his efforts and those of others like him were successful: in 1772, newspapers were allowed to print Parliamentary speeches.

The tax on knowledge

The next battle was against the 'tax on knowledge' which made newspapers too expensive for most people and forced papers to take bribes. Even *The Times*, which was started in 1785, took government bribes. However, its founder and edi-

An Illustrated London News *article on an angry meeting of the Chartists in 1866. They wanted the vote to be given to all working men. The weekly magazine was started in 1842 and was one of the first to use illustrations in news reports.*

tor, John Walter, was not afraid to criticise the government at times. Walter was fined and even went to prison for his comments on Parliament and people in power.

In 1802, Walter's son took over as manager. *The Times's* reputation for honest and fast reporting increased. As it and other papers became more successful and therefore wealthier, they began to be able to refuse some bribes. They became more independent of the rich and powerful people who had paid them in the past.

The Times, *1805. The price was sixpence (about 40p in modern money, almost twice as much as it costs today).*

In 1817, Thomas Barnes became editor. *The Times* became a newspaper respected not just in Britain but all over the world. Barnes was able to stop accepting bribes altogether. However, by now the Stamp Tax on papers had been put up to fourpence a sheet. There were also taxes on paper itself and on advertisements in papers. This meant that the price of a daily paper—the equivalent of about 40p today—was far too high for most working people. Many people were angry about this. They believed that it was everyone's right to know what was going on in the rest of their country and in the wider world. They risked fines, imprisonment and even *transportation* to publish 'unstamped'—and therefore cheap—papers.

---

4. **Why did some people start to publish unstamped papers?**

These unstamped papers began to argue increasingly for political changes, including the right for all working men to vote. One newspaper was called *Poor Man's Guardian*. 'Knowledge is Power' was printed across the front page. The first issue stated that 'we will begin by protecting and upholding ... this key to all our liberties, the freedom of the Press'. The editor believed that the rich and powerful deliberately kept other people ignorant of how the country was run and of what went on in the world. Because they could not vote, working people had no voice in the way the country was governed. How could they get Parliament to improve their working and living conditions if they did not know how to make such changes?

---

5. **Explain the slogan 'Knowledge is Power' in a few sentences. Why do you think the editor chose it for the *Poor Man's Guardian*?**

The Chartists

In 1832, Parliament passed a Reform Act but it changed very little. The poor still had no vote. Many working people joined together to form a movement called the Chartists and began demanding the vote. They supported the fight for 'untaxed knowledge'. It was a long battle. The government reduced the Advertisement Tax in 1833 but it was a further 20 years before they abolished it. The Stamp Tax was finally removed in 1855 and in 1861 the last tax, on newsprint, was abolished.

---

6. **Why would a movement like the Chartists support freedom of the Press?**

7. **How do you think the removal of the taxes affected (a) the cost and (b) the sales of newspapers?**

8. **Put the correct ending with each sentence:**
   1. The publishers of unstamped papers refused to ...
   2. They published unstamped papers so that poor people could ...
   3. The Chartists believed that working people should ...
   4. In 1855 Parliament agreed to ...
      (a) ... be able to vote.
      (b) ... remove the Stamp Tax.
      (c) ... read the news.
      (d) ... pay the Stamp Tax.

Chapter 4 The Press Gains Power

The success of the battle against the taxes on newspapers was a sign of the growing freedom and power of the Press. Without taxes, papers cost less. So their *circulations* rose and they made more money. Social, industrial and technical changes also contributed to the growth of the newspaper industry in the nineteenth century.

Social change

In 1867, many working men gained the vote. Naturally, they wanted to know more about the political issues of their time. When the taxes were finally abolished, not only did the established papers greatly increase their sales, but new papers were started—in particular, ones which included stories and information of interest to working people. A new reading public was growing up, too. The Education Act of 1870 meant that more children of working people were going to school and learning to read. Britain gradually became a nation of newspaper readers, rich and poor.

5. This illustration is from a working man's magazine of the 1860s. The father is reading a national newspaper. Give two reasons why this would have been unlikely earlier.

1. After the newspaper taxes were abolished, there was a new kind of reader. Who were they?

2. How did the Education Act of 1870 affect the newspaper industry?

During the nineteenth century, the British public began to recognise the important role the Press can play for society's good. In the 1850s, *The Times* sent William Russell, England's first war correspondent, to the Crimean War. He described the battles and told the truth about the terrible conditions suffered by ordinary soldiers.

'The wretched beggar who wandered about the streets of London in the rain led the life of a prince compared with the British soldiers who were fighting for their country, and who, we were *complacently* assured by the home authorities, were the best *appointed* army in Europe.... The persons really *culpable* were those who sent them out without a proper staff and without the smallest *foresight* ...'

3. To what does Russell compare the soldiers' condition?

4. Whom does Russell blame for their misery?

Russell's reports revealed the inefficiency of the authorities and caused a public outcry. The army was forced to make changes. Florence Nightingale, amongst others, was sent out to improve the care of the sick and wounded. Many lives were saved. Russell was called a hero. The public had a new respect for newspaper correspondents and recognised the value of 'investigative reporting'. 'Investigative reporting' means journalists seeking out and revealing injustices or incompetence that they feel the public ought to know about. In this way, the Press can sometimes change events and make news, as well as reporting it.

'He *incurred* much *enmity*, but few *unprejudiced* men who were in the Crimea will now attempt to call in question the fact that by awakening the conscience of the British nation to the sufferings of its troops, he saved the *remnant* of those grand battalions we landed in September.'

(Field Marshall Sir Evelyn Wood)

6. Why did Russell's reports about the war make him some enemies? Who might not have been pleased by them?

7. In what way did Russell's reports 'save' the lives of the 'grand battalions'?

The Railway Age

During the nineteenth century, many machines, including the steam engine, were invented. They greatly increased Britain's industrial production. From the 1830s, a railway network spread rapidly, linking towns and factories throughout the country. People were no longer restricted to local goods—nor local news, for national papers now could be quickly delivered all over the country.

British industry did well, and so did the people who owned the shops, factories and businesses that were making so much money. Train travel for business and pleasure appealed to them. A certain Mr W. H. Smith saw the potential of all these people needing something to do on their journey. In 1848, he opened a bookstall at London's Euston Station, selling newspapers, 'railway novels' and magazines. It was a huge success. Soon there were W. H. Smith bookstalls at all major stations.

---

8. **Name two ways in which the spread of the railways helped the newspaper industry.**

A telephone exchange, 1900. A reporter could now telephone his office from the spot to give his story.

Technical changes

Speed and accuracy are vital to newspaper reporting. Several inventions in the nineteenth century gave journalists the chance greatly to improve both.

Date	Invention	Advantage
1827	Much more efficient, rotary (turning) printing press, using a steam engine, invented	Newspapers can be printed faster and so can have more pages
1837	Sir Isaac Pitman develops a particularly effective system of shorthand	Reporters can take down words as quickly as they are spoken
1837	First practical electric telegraph system in operation	Exchange of news much faster, no longer dependent on human or pigeon message carriers
1873	First satisfactory typewriter made	Printers no longer need to struggle to make sense of a reporter's handwritten copy
1876	Alexander Graham Bell invents the telephone	
1879	First mechanical typesetting machine introduced	Metal letters no longer positioned by hand, so production is much faster

---

9. **Complete the 'Advantage' section for the telephone in the chart above.**

---

10. **Find out more about three of these inventions. Write a paragraph about each one, explaining how they affected the speed and/or accuracy with which the news could be printed.**

Until the mid-nineteenth century, newspapers were illustrated only with an occasional line drawing. In 1842, *The Illustrated London News*, a weekly magazine, was launched. It contained 30 illustrations. From then on, pictures became an increasingly important way in which people received their news and formed their views about the world. By the end of the century, printing methods had been developed that enabled newspapers to use photographs instead of drawings.

---

11. **There is a page from *The Illustrated London News* in Chapter 3. How does it differ from that of *The Times* in the same chapter? What do the drawings add to the news report about the Chartists?**

Chapter 5   The Popular Press

Sunday newspapers began in the early 1800s and were soon successful. Both *The Sunday Times* and the *The Observer* had many readers by the 1840s. However, *The Times* continued to sell more copies than all its rivals until the Stamp Tax was abolished in 1855. The day the tax ended, the *Daily Telegraph* was founded. It was cheaper than *The Times* and began to sell more copies.

The real change in newspaper publishing began in 1896, when William Harmsworth (later Lord Northcliffe) started the *Daily Mail*. He promised 'All the news for half the price'. He wanted to attract the mass of ordinary people who found *The Times* and the other papers too expensive or too serious and hard to understand. *The Times* had a lot of text and very few pictures. There were long articles about politics and foreign affairs.

Northcliffe changed the look, content and price of newspapers. He *popularised* the news. He presented it in a lively way, in simple language, with lots of illustrations and big headlines. He included articles about sport, fashion and crime. He was able to keep the price down to one halfpenny by making lots of money selling advertising space in the paper.

The importance of advertising

Advertising had become big business since the coming of the railways. Goods with a brand name (Lipton's Tea, Pear's Soap) could now be transported and sold all over the country. Manufacturers wanted people everywhere to recognise and buy their products. Northcliffe was able to persuade many of them to advertise in the *Daily Mail* because the paper's style attracted plenty of readers. By 1900, the *Daily Mail* had a circulation of over a million. The newspaper industry had become very profitable. In 1900 and 1903 two competitors were launched: the *Daily Express* and the *Daily Mirror*.

---

1.   In what way did the railways help
     (a) the manufacturers of branded goods and
     (b) Lord Northcliffe?

---

2.   Why do you think the *Daily Mail*, *Daily Express* and *Daily Mirror* were called the 'popular' Press?

A Victorian advertisement.

---

3.   In what ways did the *Daily Mail* look different from the earlier national newspapers?

Lord Northcliffe's successful introduction of advertising into newspapers was the first of many changes in the industry. Sales went up but the number of different newspapers published went down. At the same time, they were owned by fewer and fewer people. By 1929, almost half of Britain's dailies were owned by just four businessmen. Circulations continued to grow until after the Second World War. Then labour and printing costs started to rise, particularly in the 1960s and 1970s. Papers became more expensive to produce. Prices went up and people cut down on the number they bought.

Since the 1920s, the newspaper industry has also had to compete with other mass media. Radio and television have become increasingly popular sources of daily news and information. In addition, television has attracted more and more advertisers, taking them away from newspapers. Very few national newspapers have made a profit in recent years.

The newspaper revolution?

An important part of *The Times*'s success during the nineteenth century was the owners' great interest in developing more efficient methods of

4. **Look at the pages of the *Daily Mail* (1908) reproduced here. List three things about them which illustrate Lord Northcliffe's ideas about newspaper publishing.**

printing. The use of new printing *technology* is still the most crucial issue facing the newspaper industry today. Three major printing revolutions have taken place in the last ten years, all involving computers. It is now possible for a journalist to write, *edit* and print an article all on one machine. Computer technology has also made it possible for newspapers to use colour photographs to illustrate their stories, and it is now much cheaper to start up and run a newspaper. This means that more new titles can be launched, giving the reading public a wider choice. *Today*, launched in 1986, was the first national daily newspaper to make full use of computer technology, and to print coloured photographs. Other new papers followed. It is too early to say how successful these new ventures will be.

There are problems, however. Using the new technology means changing and losing many jobs, particularly in the printing industry. Understandably, the printworkers' unions are unhappy about this. There have been bitter disputes, strikes and talks. The unions and newspaper management have yet to agree on the best way to deal with the issue.

Also, the new papers have to win readers and advertisers away from the established titles, which is very difficult. People tend to be very slow to change their reading habits. Nonetheless, there is no doubt that the newspaper industry is going through considerable change.

5. **Do you think that the newspaper page reproduced below looks more interesting than the page of *The Times* shown on page 9? If so, explain why in a few sentences.**

Chapter 6   The Press Today

More daily papers are sold per person in Britain than almost anywhere in the world. The national papers have a combined circulation of 15 million on weekdays and over 18 million on Sundays—and most copies are read by several people.

One result of the competition from radio and television is that modern papers offer readers more than news. They contain information and views about the arts, articles on such matters as housing and education, fashion features, gossip columns and competitions. Some papers contain almost more entertainment than news. Most Sunday papers include a colour magazine.

Certain papers are known for their investigative journalism. One example was when *The Sunday Times* revealed important facts about the drug Thalidomide in 1976. This had caused deformities in babies. In America, the *Washington Post* investigated the 'buggings' in the Watergate block of flats. They discovered information that involved President Nixon, which eventually forced him to resign in 1974.

1.   **What is investigative reporting?**

2.   **Give an example of some early investigative reporting, in the nineteenth century.**

Quality and popular press

People often speak of the national Press as being divided into 'quality' and 'popular' papers. Two extreme examples would be the *Financial Times* (quality) and the *Sun* (popular). The chart below lists in a simple way the style of writing and the kinds of subjects found in these two groups.

Most national papers are not connected with any of Britain's political parties but they may support a particular political point of view. One good reason for having papers with different styles and content is that they present a variety of arguments and views on current affairs. On the whole, however, people tend to read the paper which expresses views that they agree with. In other words, they buy the one which gives them the news they want, the way they want it. For example, the *Daily Telegraph* (quality) appeals to more conservative readers than the *Guardian* (quality).

3.   **What is the advantage of having newspapers with different political points of view?**

So much is happening every day, all over the world, that newspapers couldn't gather all the news with just their own staff. They rely on news agencies for certain kinds of information. These are organisations that gather and distribute news to papers, and television and radio companies. There are three big agencies in Britain. One, Reuters, dates from the 1890s, when Paul Reuter started a news service using pigeons. Today, Reuters provides international news, the Press Association deals with home news and Extel deals with finance and sport. British papers also use two American agencies, Associated Press and United Press International.

Every day, hundreds of news stories and pictures pour into a newspaper's office. Some are so 'newsworthy' that they will appear in every paper—for example, an important meeting between politicans, a major sporting event or a disaster of some kind. The editor and his or her staff then go through all the remaining news and decide what else to include.

By leaving out some stories and selecting others—or by giving more or less importance to certain stories—an editor can affect our view of current events. This is known as 'selective editing'. Journalists give importance to a story by (a) size of headline, (b) length of text, (c) illustration, and (d) position in the paper. A headline can affect the reader's whole view of an item. So can a photograph.

THE GUARDIAN

Quality
serious
lots of text

national news
foreign news
economics
politics
arts
crosswords
letters on current affairs

Popular
lively
lots of pictures
national news
crime
sport
entertainment
gossip
cartoons
competitions

4. Do the two headlines on the left present the same view of the event? How are they different?

The dangerous thing about photographs is that they are often accepted as 'true' because they appear to be a record of what actually happened. Yet they can be used just as selectively as words to strengthen the point the paper wants to make. For example, an editor may print a picture of the one violent incident in an otherwise peaceful demonstration.

5. Why do you think that an editor might do this?

6. Describe what is meant by selective editing.

7. Find out the history of your local newspaper. When was it founded? Who started it? Who owns it now? Have there been any important incidents, such as clashes with the local council over the way a story was reported? You could display this information in your classroom, as a frieze.

8. This is a rather extreme example of how a quality and a popular paper treated the news on the same day. Examine the emphasis they give to the one main story they both cover. Describe how they differ in their treatment of it and of the news generally.

Chapter 7 The Power of the Press

Today, many of Britain's newspapers are owned by a few large companies, such as News International. There are also a few individual owners. In the early days of the newspaper industry, some politicians and businessmen tried to use the printed word to support their own interests and expand their power. Newspapers no longer take bribes from individuals or political parties, as they did 100 years ago. People are more aware of the need to protect the freedom of the Press. There is also more awareness of the power which the Press has and of the danger of this being wrongly used.

The Press Council

In 1953, the Press Council was set up. It makes sure that newspapers do not publish material that is 'not in the public interest'—for example, how to commit the perfect burglary. Disputes about the freedom of the Press can be taken to the Council. So can complaints about the way that an incident has been reported.

The article on the right describes how Manchester City Council complained to the Press Council about a *Sunday Times* investigation into the way an old people's home was run. The report said that the conditions in the home were 'inhuman' and that the council had failed to improve them. The city council said that the report was 'grossly inaccurate and misleading'. The Press Council decided that the city council's complaints were unfounded and that 'such investigations are ... in the public interest'.

1. **What was the role of the Press Council in this argument?**

2. **Why do you think the Press Council felt that the investigation was in the public interest?**

Some people feel that because the Press Council is made up of newspaper people, it might favour a newspaper's case against a complaint from outside the industry. Should there be a more powerful 'watchdog' than the Press Council, perhaps the government? The danger is that it is only a short step from banning material because it might offend or endanger people, to banning it for political reasons. For example, a government might use such powers to ban publication of bad trade or unemployment figures because these would make it unpopular. This is why many people argue in favour of self-censorship—like the newspaper industry's Press Council—rather than government censorship.

3. **Why do people think it might be dangerous for the government to control the Press?**

4. **What are the dangers of any industry being its own 'watchdog'?**

Newspapers today do not make enough money from sales to survive. Advertisements are, in many cases, their most important source of income. Advertisements are checked by an independent organisation, called The Advertising Standards Authority. Certain kinds of advertisements which appeared in Victorian newspapers—for example, those promising miracle health cures—would no longer be allowed. They are not 'legal, decent, honest and truthful'.

5. **Why would an advertisement like this no longer be seen in a British paper?**

DR. J. COLLIS BROWNE'S CHLORODYNE
Rapidly cuts short all attacks of
EPILEPSY, PALPITATION, SPASMS, HYSTERIA, COLIC, AND IS THE TRUE PALLIATIVE IN
NEURALGIA, RHEUMATISM, GOUT, CANCER, TOOTHACHE.

Daily Mail

STEIN DIES
Back Page

WEDNESDAY, SEPTEMBER 11, 198_
20p

Two die in
● night of arson
and looting

Angry mob force
● Home Secretary
to dive for cover

Hurd warns:
● This could hit
other cities

BLOODLUST

COPYCAT RIOTS could hit other cities following the bloodshed and destruction in Handsworth, Home Secretary Douglas Hurd warned police forces yesterday.

Minutes earlier, he himself had been a target for the black mobs on the area's shattered streets and was forced to escape in a police van as bricks, bottles and other missiles rained down.

Mr Hurd was escorted to safety by West Midlands Chief Constable Mr Geoffrey Dear, who blamed the riots on hooligans—the worst elements of society driven on by a 'bloodlust'.

By GORDON GREIG, AUBREY CHALMERS and JOHN HAMSHIRE

Tense

A youth menacingly brandishes a petrol bomb... ... *and hurls it during yesterday's rioting*

6. The cover of the *Daily Mail* after the riots in Birmingham, 1985. What sort of feelings do you think the paper's headlines and picture might stir up in its readers?

A Free Press?

Britain has had for many years a reputation for a free Press, although one famous editor recently called it a 'half-free' Press. He felt that it would have been impossible for an English newspaper to have had the freedom to reveal the crimes of Watergate, as the *Washington Post* did in America.

There is no state control or censorship of what is written in British newspapers but there are certain laws which affect their *access* to information and the type of material they can publish. For example, there are restrictions on reporting certain types of court trials, such as those involving children, so as to protect the people involved. There are laws on *copyright*, which protect authors' work from being stolen, and *libel*, which protect people from damaging accusations. There are also restrictions on the publication of material which is 'dangerous to the nation's security'. These issues are not always clear-cut. Sometimes journalists feel they are being unfairly

restricted. Several times, a newspaper has gone to court to defend its right to publish certain material. During the Falklands war in 1982, some reporters felt that too many details and decisions about the fighting were being kept secret. The government, however, said that national security was at risk. They said that they couldn't reveal any more information without endangering soldiers' lives or their chances of success.

7. Sentences 1 to 4 below are examples of a, b, c and d. Put the right letter with the right sentence and write a couple of sentences about why you think there are laws about each one.

1) Printing a new novel without the author's permission.
2) Accusations that a senior politician has stolen money.
3) Secret information about Britain's defence systems.
4) Instructions on how to make a bomb or cheat the tax inspector.

(a) libel
(b) information dangerous to nation's security
(c) information not in the public interest
(d) breaking the law of copyright

In 1985, there were bad riots in some of Britain's inner cities. Some community leaders were angry with the way that the Press reported them. They felt that pictures like the one on this page simply made people more angry or frightened and did nothing to increase their understanding of what had gone wrong. The police, too, sometimes felt that the Press reported their activities unfairly and that journalists being in the riot areas made the situation worse. Here is what one editor, Donald Trelford of *The Observer*, said about the role of the Press in the riots.

'An important function of a newspaper is to inform our *democracy* by providing independent news, so that people are not wholly dependent on official sources for the facts on which they base their decisions. To do that in a rioting city means going in there ourselves.'

8. Explain in your own words Donald Trelford's reasons for sending journalists into the riot areas. Do you agree with him?

Chapter 8   Book Publishing

For centuries, books were the only means of recording and storing information. But for books to be an effective medium for educating, informing—and entertaining—the mass of people, three things are essential: (a) that writers are free to say what they think, (b) that people have the opportunity to learn to read, and (c) that everyone can afford to borrow or buy books.

At first books were copied by hand. They were rare, valuable and often beautifully decorated. Most people never even touched a book in their lives. The earliest known printed book was a Chinese prayer book of AD 868. More than 500 years later, books in Europe were still being hand copied. It was not until the fifteenth century and Gutenberg's invention that printing in Europe became relatively fast and cheap.

The first English book was printed by William Caxton in 1476. More people learnt to read but education was still only for the rich and the clergy. Books are an important source of ideas and knowledge. Through reading, people learn of the different experiences and beliefs of others. Some members of the government, the monarchy and the Church did not want ideas to spread which conflicted with their own. In the eighteenth century their efforts to control the print medium with laws and taxes included books as well as newspapers.

Writers gained more freedom to write what they wanted, however, with the 1709 Copyright Act. Before this, most writers had to find a wealthy *patron* to support them. Naturally, they had to produce work which pleased their patrons. The 1709 Act stated that writers owned the copyright on their work. Each time a copy of their writing was sold or used, they were to be paid. Writers no longer needed to depend on a patron for money. Many people still could not read, however, and books were too expensive for most working people.

Children carrying heavy clay at a brick works. Child labour was common in the nineteenth century, but after 1870 children had the right to go to school and learn to read.

cheaper. Railway station bookstalls sold thousands of cheap 'railway novels' to travellers. Some publishers were concerned about the low quality of these novels. They produced cheap but good books which were meant to help working people educate and 'improve' themselves.

Some industries, such as mining, and some big companies provided libraries for their workers. Often these were for men only. Wives had to clean, cook and look after the children after work. The Victorian ideal that women should be 'ladies of leisure' meant that books were one of the few sources of interest and entertainment for well-off women but ordinary working women had little *leisure*. They could rarely afford either the time to read or the cost of a book.

> 'The working men's wives read less than their husbands. They have no definite intervals of leisure. . . . Nearly all of them seem to have this feeling that it is wrong to sit down with a book if there is anything more practical to do.'
>
> (Lady Florence Bell, *At the Works, 1907*)

---

1. **How did the Copyright Act help writers?**

The nineteenth century

The Education Act of 1870 was the first of several acts passed by Parliament to make sure more people learnt to read. At the same time, printing methods improved and books became

---

2. **Look back at the picture on page 10. Does it fit in with Lady Bell's view? Why does she say working women have less chance to read books than their husbands?**

---

3. **Was the situation the same for all women at the time?**

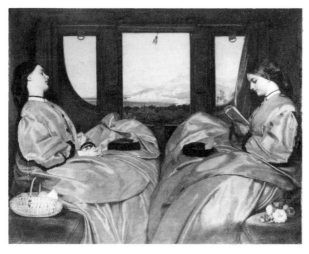

Train travel became popular after the 1830s. Long journeys encouraged people to read.

Working men reading newspapers in a Manchester library, 1862. By this time many cities had a Working Men's Library or Institute, paid for by the men themselves.

The twentieth century

By the beginning of this century, lending libraries had become very popular but few were free. Most were privately run and only those who could afford the *subscription* could use them. In 1919 a Public Libraries Act was passed which encouraged the setting up of free lending libraries all over Britain. Book borrowing was now possible for everyone.

4. Why was the 1919 Public Libraries Act important (a) to book publishers and (b) to the less well-off reader?

The paperback revolution

Book publishing faced many of the same problems as newspapers. From 1870 the book trade grew fast. After the 1930s, production costs started to go up. Small companies found it hard to make money. Then, in 1935, Penguin Books published the first of their paperbacks. Their success changed the book trade. Cheap paper books had been sold before—what made Penguin different was that they published good work. By mass-producing *fiction* and non-fiction of a high standard at a low price the company was soon making a major contribution to adult education.

5. How did paperbacks help spread ideas and knowledge among the British public?

Hardcover books are now bought mainly by schools and libraries. Most people borrow books

rather than buy them. Television is now more popular than reading as a way to relax. Books based on television programmes, or on which programmes, plays or films have been based, usually sell well. People have more leisure time and so books on all sorts of hobbies and interests have become popular.

5. How does book publishing (a) suffer and (b) gain from the rival medium of TV?

Today, computer technology has given us another means to store information. Computer information systems are replacing printed texts in some subjects, especially those which need constant updating. It may not be long before large reference books, such as the *Encyclopaedia Britannica*, are put on computer.

6. Do you think that storing information on computer instead of in books will make it more or less available to the majority of people?

7. Re-read the first paragraph. Name three Acts of Parliament which helped bring about points (a), (b) and (c) and describe how they affected the publishing industry.

Despite competition from other media, the number of books published continues to rise.

Chapter 9   Magazines

A magazine is a regular publication which contains articles by various writers. The first magazines were started in the seventeenth century, first in France and later in England and Germany. The name comes from 'magasin', a French word meaning a general store. Magazines soon became popular. Like newspapers, they were badly affected by the Stamp Tax, but new ones continued to appear. They were full of news, public information, extracts from books and plays, letters and entertaining articles on a wide range of subjects.

---

1.   What does the name magazine come from? Why do you think they were called that? The contents of the magazine opposite should tell you.

By the early 1800s, literary magazines were well established. These published new work by important poets and writers. At the same time, cheaper, more popular magazines began to appear. These appealed to the growing numbers of ordinary working people drawn to the cities by jobs in factories and mills. By the end of the century, such magazines were very successful. The development of advertising had made them more profitable. They now had the technology to print photographs. Illustrated news magazines were particularly popular. People were better educated, communications were faster and there was more interest in world affairs.

---

2.   Describe some developments in the nineteenth century that helped to expand the audience for magazines.

Throughout the twentieth century, people's leisure time has gradually increased. Laws protect them from working long hours. Labour-saving machines mean many jobs now take less time to do. Many of the 6000 magazines and journals published in Britain today are written for people with hobbies and special interests. They cover a huge range of subjects—from computers to cats and rock music to rock gardens.

There are also many technical journals, for people in different industries and professions,

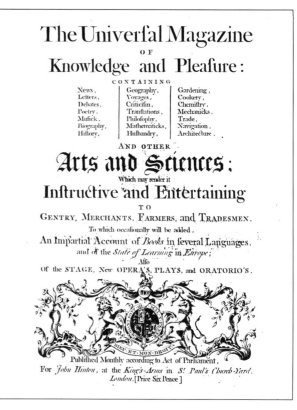

A magazine of 1748. There are articles on many different subjects.

from farming to science. Scientific and scholarly magazines began in the nineteenth century, which was a time of great discovery and technical progress. Today, technology is developing so quickly that people constantly need up-to-date information. Magazines are an ideal medium for this.

---

3.   Books are available on all the subjects covered by magazines. Why do you think that people want magazines as well?

Children's comics

Each week, about 1½ million comics are sold. Several of the most popular sell more copies than *The Times*! The first children's comics began around the 1780s. They were rather serious. They were meant to 'improve' and educate. In the nineteenth century, they became more fun. They contained adventure stories, school and detective *serials*, as well as information on scientific marvels, history, geography and sport. As books for children became cheaper, there was less of a need for the 'educational' comic. Books were for learning; comics were for entertainment. Comic strips full of action and pictures became popular.

---

4. Why did cheaper books mean that educational comics became less popular?

The content of comics has changed over the years. Today, children are entertained by other mass media. Comic stories about television series and film characters are particularly successful. Space and science fiction are subjects that are attracting more and more readers. Stories about the two World Wars are finally losing their appeal.

---

5. What effect have the modern media had on the content of children's comics?

Sexism and racism in the media

Fashion and pop music are very popular today, even with young children. A lot of fashion and pop 'news' is directed at girls. Boys' comics contain more science fiction, war, sport and 'action' stories. This can mean that girls and boys start reading different comics from a young age. Many people feel that this adds to the problem of girls and boys being made to feel that their interests are quite different.

We get most of our information and explanation about the world we live in from the media. Their content can shape our views. If programmes and publications for women and girls deal largely with fashion, cookery, pop and film news and gossip, love and romance, they can seem to be saying that these are the only things women like to think about.

Women's magazines began in the eighteenth century but really became popular in the following century. At this time the 'ideal' woman was one whose only concern was to create the perfect home for her family. Magazines were full of advice about how to do this. Today, many women's magazines have changed. They recognise that the majority of women work and have interests outside the home. They tackle difficult or 'serious' issues which were avoided before. Girls' comics, however, often tell a different story.

6. Look at the covers of *Girl* magazine (1951) and *Mandy* (1986) (above). Which one presents girls with the most adventurous picture of themselves?

There is a similar danger of the media encouraging false ideas about Britain's different racial groups. An example would be comic stories or television programmes in which the heroes and heroines are always white. If black children never see someone of their own colour on TV doing something exciting or adventurous or, for example, being a teacher or doctor, this can give the impression that such activities are not for them. Children today receive so much of their information and entertainment through the mass media that it is very important that the media do not present them with misleading or discouraging ideas about their place in society.

7. Explain in your own words the point this cartoonist is making.

Chapter 10 The Electronic Mass Media

'The printing press, which multiplies the word of the thinker; the steam engine, which both feeds the press and rushes off with its product; and the electric telegraph, which carries thought around the globe, make this an age in which mental force assumes an importance which it had never had before in the history of mankind.' (M. Fenwick Miller)

1. Rewrite the sentence in your own words.

2. This was written in the 1880s. Why did the writer feel the power of thought had more importance than it had ever had before?

3. Name two media, invented since this was written, which also carry 'thought around the globe'.

Fenwick Miller was writing at a time when the printed word was the major means of mass communication. The print media (the newspaper and publishing industries) have existed for centuries. The electronic media (radio, cinema and television) are much more recent. They were invented in this century, long after Britain had undergone its Industrial Revolution. Radio and television, in particular, needed the mass city audiences and the technological skills which had been produced by that 'revolution'.

The Industrial Revolution

Between 1760 and 1840, the use of new machinery, materials and methods of transport slowly changed Britain from an agricultural society to an industrial one. Between 1800 and 1850, the population doubled. Thousands of people moved from country areas to the cities, where the jobs were. Industry was booming and it was based in the towns, which were now linked by the railways. Britain was no longer a country of scattered towns and villages. By the end of the nineteenth century, huge numbers of people were concentrated together in ever-growing cities. Their children were going to state-funded schools. Scientific and technical knowledge was expanding fast. The telegraph, the telephone and then the wireless were invented. The skills to develop the electronic media were emerging and the mass audiences for them now existed. People were better educated than ever before and were eager for information and entertainment.

4. In what way did events during the nineteenth century create conditions that were ideal for the development of the mass media of radio and television?

5. The word 'broadcasting' means 'to scatter or sow over a wide area'. Why do you think this word is used to describe the transmitting of programmes by radio and television?

Workers' 'cottages', 1870. By the end of the nineteenth century Britain's cities had grown enormously. Thousands of people had moved from the country in order to find jobs in industry.

Broadcasting to the masses

Cinemas were in existence before radio but radio was the first of the electronic media to achieve mass audiences. It was invented for a purely practical purpose: to meet the need for fast, long-distance communications. Yet its development changed people's lives. Radio programmes gave British people access to more knowledge and information than previous generations could have imagined possible. Radio played a crucial part in the great social changes which Britain went through in the first half of the twentieth century, after World War One. Along with the motor car, the aeroplane, the use of advertising and the ever-expanding newspaper industry, radio helped to change dramatically the pattern of communications. People's interests and expectations rapidly expanded as they learnt more about the world around them.

This is how one woman, a London office cleaner, described the importance of radio to her in 1939:

'I think radio's a proper education. Wireless makes learning easy. The people talking might be in the same room ... there's the news and the talks by famous people about what is going on in the world. ... Twenty years ago a woman like me wouldn't know anything about politics, but thanks to the radio I can hold my own quite well.'

(Florence Knightly, interviewed in *The Radio Times*, 1939)

---

6. Describe the difference that listening to the radio made to this woman.

A LOST ART.

THE DINNER-PARTIES OF OUR ANCESTORS WERE EMBELLISHED WITH SPARKLING CONVERSATION—

BUT NOWADAYS THE TALKING IS DONE "OFF"

One by one, inventions and discoveries were made and the modern media evolved. Usually it took time for the public to accept a new medium or to accept new developments in an old one. People often worried that the new medium would destroy other forms of social communication and entertainment. Here are some of the arguments that have been put forward over the years:

1) The printed word will destroy the art of conversation.
2) Radio will stop people going out to concerts and plays.
3) Radio's news service means that no-one will buy evening papers.
4) Television viewing requires so little effort compared to listening to the radio or reading a book, that no-one will bother to do either any more.
5) Advertising on television means the end of good programmes.
6) Breakfast television will take away the audience from morning radio.

In 1930, the Bishop of Hereford said that he feared that broadcasting made people give up doing things for themselves:

'It will be a bad day for England if people become content to look on at football and not play, or listen to wireless and not sing.'

E. V. Lucas, who was a well known writer, said in 1924 that 'broadcasting is the death of conversation and *repose*'.

---

7. What does the last quotation mean? Do you agree with it, or with any of the other statements above? Write a few sentences about those which you feel have come true in some ways.

---

8. It is often said today that computers and video equipment will replace books. Do you agree? Give reasons for your opinion.

---

9. What point is the *Punch* cartoonist making (left)? Would he have agreed with E. V. Lucas?

This cartoon appeared in Punch *in 1923, in the early days of radio. The guests in the lower picture are wearing the kind of headphones they needed to 'listen in' at that time. ('Embellished' means 'decorated'.)*

23

Chapter 11 Look! No Wires

The speed of long-distance communications was greatly improved by the invention of telegraphic equipment in 1792. In 1837 an electric telegraph system was developed which worked by sending an electrical current down a wire which connected two machines: a transmitter and a receiver.

In 1899, a young Italian living in Britain, Guglielmo Marconi, succeeded in sending a message across to France without using wires. He had discovered a way of *transmitting* sound using invisible energy waves in the air. In 1901, he sent a message from Cornwall to America. It was then that the Armed Forces recognised the great possibilities of the 'wireless'—what we call radio. During World War One (1914–1918), radio was used to keep aeroplanes, army patrols, ships and submarines in vital touch with each other.

---

1. **Why do you think Marconi's invention was called the 'wireless'?**

2. **Why would the wireless be so much more useful than the telegraph for armed forces on the move?**

Two dramatic incidents brought radio to the public's attention. In 1910, the notorious murderer Dr Crippen was discovered on a ship trying to escape from Britain. The ship's captain used his radio to alert the police (see page 13). Two years later, the giant passenger ship *Titanic* struck an iceberg and sank. The wireless operator sent out desperate S.O.S. signals. These were heard by ships 80 kilometres (50 miles) away, which arrived in time to rescue 20 boatloads of passengers.

The BBC

Although fiddling with wireless sets was a hobby for hundreds of amateur radio enthusiasts, there was no regular radio service to listen to until the 1920s. In 1920, Lord Northcliffe of the *Daily Mail* suggested broadcasting a special concert with Dame Nellie Melba, a famous singer. It was a great success and was heard all over Europe. However, the Post Master General banned such broadcasts because they would interfere with 'important communications'. The wireless societies protested and in 1922 the ban was lifted.

SHOOT MAN SHOOT

Tense with excitement . . . . thrilled. Almost seeing the game, so clearly does he hear it. Can you wonder that he shouts? Such radio is new to him. It comes as a revelation that broadcasting can be so vividly alive. It is his new Pye Portable—the portable supreme. Entirely self-contained — ready always for immediate use, anywhere. Glorious in tone, generous in volume, comprehensive in range of reception.

The Pye Portable is so well worth hearing that you owe it to yourself to go to your radio dealer at once for a demonstration. He will tell you of the magnificent reputation of the Pye Portable and of the lasting satisfaction it brings to its users.

The finest quality radio in the World—now so easy to buy! The Pye Portable can be yours for the first of 12 monthly payments of 35/- (The cash price is now only £19.19.0)

Dual wavelength range; single dial tuning with fast and slow motion control calibrated in wavelengths. A wonderful receiver in a beautifully hand-polished walnut cabinet.

PYE PORTABLE RADIO
—MADE IN CAMBRIDGE—

One of the pleasures of the new medium of radio was that it allowed people to listen to events as they took place. This 1930 advertisement emphasises this, saying that the listener is 'Almost seeing the game, so clearly does he hear it'.

Several firms who made and sold radio equipment formed the British Broadcasting Company. Their first daily broadcast was on 14 November, 1922. Listeners had to buy a radio licence from the Post Office. Many of the early programmes were made up of news and useful information.

For those who had never come across radio before, it seemed quite miraculous. This is how one woman described it:

'I went round to my next-door neighbour's house and I saw this round *cone . . .* on the wall. And I went into my mother and I said "Mother, Mrs Buckle's wall is singing". "Don't talk so silly", she says. So I says, "There is, there's some music coming out of the wall!"'
(*Those Radio Times*)

---

3. **Imagine that you have just heard a radio for the first time. Write a letter to a friend describing what it was like.**

It was through radio that millions of people started to appreciate classical music.

It took time for radio to be accepted. At first, the news had to be read at 7.00 pm, so that it would not affect the sales of evening papers. In 1923, the Dean of Westminster refused to allow the wedding service of the Duke of York to be broadcast, in case it might be heard in 'an irreverent manner and even by persons in a public house with their hats on'. However, by 1924 there were more than a million licence holders.

4. **Why was the newspaper industry worried by the new medium of radio?**

In 1926 there was a General Strike. Many important unions refused to work and no newspapers were printed. The government used the BBC to keep people informed of events and radio won many new listeners.

5. **Why do you think radio was important during the General Strike for (a) the government and (b) the general public?**

A cartoon about radio broadcasts during the General Strike.

The wonder of the wireless

In 1927, the government took over the BBC and renamed it the British Broadcasting Corporation.

By 1939, 8 out of every 10 families were regular radio listeners. Today, it is perhaps hard to imagine just what a dramatic change radio made to people's lives. It opened the door to a world of *culture* and entertainment for many families who rarely, if ever, had the chance to visit a theatre, concert, or great public event. They could listen to dance bands, comedy shows and sporting events. Radio gave many people who had not had the chance of much education, the opportunity to discover the work of great writers and composers, famous actors, singers and musicians. As one music critic said: 'A plain man can get within two or three years a knowledge of masterpieces which his father could scarcely have acquired in a lifetime.' Radio also kept people in touch with current affairs and political discussion.

6. **In what ways did radio make British people of the 1930s more informed and knowledgeable than ever before?**

7. **What could radio bring to people that newspapers could not?**

The BBC's programmes reflected the views of John Reith, its general manager. He believed that broadcasting's duty was to widen people's interests and educate them, rather than just to entertain. For example, he felt that *Children's Hour* should contain 'a sprinkling of information attractively conveyed'. It should help children to develop their imaginations. Children were told that they would get the best enjoyment from the wireless 'only if you are prepared to give an item your full concentration'.

8. **Which of the following statements would John Reith have agreed with?**
   (a) '*Children's Hour* should provide only enjoyment.'
   (b) 'Using your imagination helps you get the best out of the programmes.'
   (c) 'Listening to *Children's Hour* takes no effort or concentration.'
   (d) '*Children's Hour* should inform as well as entertain you.'

Chapter 12   A Nation of Listeners

Using the imagination was seen as an important part of radio listening for adults as well as children. John Reith said that 'the success of the radio play depends upon the listener', because their imagination provides the pictures. Radio drama became very popular. Many famous writers wrote specially for the wireless. The BBC was also very fond of broadcasting 'talks'. These ranged from amusing ones to serious political lectures. Some people complained that there were too many '*highbrow*' talks, full of information meant to 'improve' the listener.

---

1.   What did John Reith mean by 'the success of the radio play depends upon the listener'?

Many listeners liked the way that radio put them in touch with great public events and ceremonies which normally they could only have read about in the papers. Now they could listen to the King or the Prime Minister as they made an important speech. Often several families, sometimes whole streets, came together to listen to an important broadcast. In 1937, the BBC broadcast the coronation of King George VI. It was heard all over the world and helped British citizens throughout the Empire to feel part of the occasion.

Here are some comments by radio listeners in the 1930s:

'The BBC often forgets about the ordinary working public, especially when arranging talks and discussions. So many of them are . . . right outside ordinary people's interests.'   (Housewife)

'The BBC is wasting its enormous opportunities of influencing the cultural life of the people by lowering its standards to meet popular tastes.' (Student)

'I'm a "lowbrow" really, but I like to hear serious talks. . . . The BBC is giving us plenty of knowledge to take in. You're bringing the listener up in his standard of music.'   (Engineer)

'People in general, and country people in particular, look to radio as their link with the world of progress and events.'   (Journalist)

'The church I attend is four miles away and sometimes in winter . . . it is not easy to get there. When

Comedy programmes were very popular. This shows Charlie Chester and other radio stars of the 1940s.

we cannot go, the wireless brings our worship to our fireside. That's one of the things we enjoy most of all.'   (Farmer's wife)

'If the wireless weren't there I'd miss it for one thing—big events and the chance of hearing people I'd never otherwise hear—Roosevelt's speech, for example.'   (Civil Servant)

'Broadcasting is the people's entertainment. Well-to-do people don't give a rap for it. They've got plenty of other pleasures. . . . We want programmes that touch our lives.'   (Plumber)

'I would cater for the majority every time . . . not everyone pays to be compulsorily educated.'
(Housewife)

'Radio should be an education, but it isn't. There is not enough first-rate material.'   (Teacher)

'I like the dance music and the Variety shows . . . they make you think you are laughing with the people watching the show.'   (Sailor)
(*The Radio Times*, 1939)

---

2.   Read these listeners' comments carefully and, in your own words, list their likes and dislikes in two columns, headed 'Good' and 'Bad'.

World War Two

In 1936, the world's first regular television service was broadcast in London. Radio had a rival. But three years later World War Two broke out. The television service was shut down, and radio remained Britain's main source of news. Over half of Britain's population listened anxiously to the *Nine o'Clock News* every night. The Prime Minister's speeches were broadcast on radio. So were war correspondents' first-hand reports. The public became increasingly tired of the war as they struggled to cope with food and clothes rationing, air raids, and long working hours. Radio encouraged them by providing them with laughter and *escapism*. Plays, comedies, and musical and variety shows helped to keep people cheerful.

There was another side to wartime radio. Governments used it to spread *propaganda*, that is, to put across a particular message. The Nazi government in Germany used to transmit news in English which could be received in Britain. It was always bad from the British point of view. However, since the British government wished to encourage people, their broadcasts tended to look on the bright side. Some people said that if you listened to both and imagined something in between, you probably got close to the truth.

When the war ended, television returned but radios still outnumbered TV sets by millions. The Light Programme (1945)—now Radio 2—and the Third Programme (1946)—now Radio 3—were introduced. Audiences had a far wider choice of listening. Gradually, however, more families could afford television. In 1953, the coronation of Queen Elizabeth II was broadcast on both media. For the first time, a television audience (20 million) exceeded a radio audience (12 million).

3. **Why do you think that more people chose to watch the coronation than to listen to it?**

Satellites and space

The invention of the tiny transistor valve in 1948 made radios more popular again. It meant that radios could be smaller and cheaper. Several members of the same family could have their own set and listen to different programmes.

In the 1960s, it was discovered that television, radio, telephone and computer signals from earth could be bounced off satellites in space to receiving stations millions of miles away. By now, television was well established and viewers could choose between BBC and ITV. Most people listened to radio during the day, before television came on.

Also in the 1960s, 'pirate' radio stations playing continuous pop music won many listeners. They often transmitted from ships moored outside *territorial waters* to avoid Britain's laws about broadcasting. New laws were introduced to stop them but they had taught the BBC a lesson. In 1967, it launched its own pop music station (Radio 1) and gained many young listeners.

4. **What did the pirate stations tell the BBC about its audience?**

In the early years of radio and during the war, people often got together to listen to important speeches and public events.

Chapter 13 Radio Today

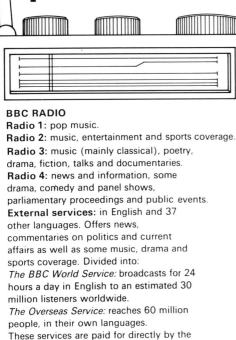

BBC RADIO
Radio 1: pop music.
Radio 2: music, entertainment and sports coverage.
Radio 3: music (mainly classical), poetry, drama, fiction, talks and documentaries.
Radio 4: news and information, some drama, comedy and panel shows, parliamentary proceedings and public events.
External services: in English and 37 other languages. Offers news, commentaries on politics and current affairs as well as some music, drama and sports coverage. Divided into:
The BBC World Service: broadcasts for 24 hours a day in English to an estimated 30 million listeners worldwide.
The Overseas Service: reaches 60 million people, in their own languages.
These services are paid for directly by the government, which determines the languages and length of the broadcasts but not the content.

You can listen to the radio wherever you are, whatever you are doing.

In 1967, the BBC opened the first of its local radio stations. The aim was to increase community feeling. Families were generally better off than before the war but many people felt that neighbours were now less ready to help each other or to build up a friendly community spirit. Local radio concentrates on local news and services—such as job vacancies, public events, and matters like new motorways, which might affect the community.

The BBC now has 30 local radio stations. There are also 43 Independent Local Radio stations. Together, they serve about 90 per cent of the population. More are planned. They cover local and regional news and information, entertainment, education, and consumer affairs. Many have 'phone-ins' so that people get a chance to give their views about all sorts of matters.

---

1. **A community is a group of people who belong together because of where they live, the beliefs they share or some other link. How do you think the medium of local radio could help to build up community spirit in the area it covers? Here are some suggestions:**
    (a) **It makes people more aware of local events.**
    (b) **It helps people feel they have something in common with others in the community.**
    (c) **It encourages people to get involved in local politics.**
    (d) **It gives local people a chance to say what they feel about the way the community is run.**
    (e) **It can act as a voice for people in the community.**
    Add some more suggestions of your own.

---

2. **Design a poster and/or write a letter which sums up your reasons for supporting the setting up of a local radio service in your community.**

Radio worldwide

In many parts of the world, radio is still the most widespread means of mass communication. In country areas of Asia, Africa and South America, it has proved a powerful medium for education, as well as for providing information and entertainment. Throughout the world, it remains the fastest means of spreading news. At times of crisis, people often switch on the radio first for up-to-date newsflashes and turn to the television later for fuller, illustrated coverage.

Radio also has the advantage of being easy to transmit over very long distances. Television can do this only with the aid of satellites. Thus governments who try to control or even shut down broadcasting in their own countries have

Radio is an effective medium for education, especially in remote country areas. These farmers in Mali are listening to farming news and advice.

Talking to people in the community is an important part of local radio programmes.

great difficulty in preventing people from tuning into information transmitted by radio from other countries. The Soviet Union, America and China all have large foreign service broadcasting operations, like BBC radio's external services.

---

3. **If your country was suddenly invaded by a foreign power, why would the chance to listen to a radio be important? Would television or the newspapers be as important a source of information? Give reasons for your answer.**

---

4. **What advantage could there be in hearing news broadcasts from another country?**

Radio keeps its audience

Great changes have taken place in the communication media in the last two decades. Television is now the main source of entertainment for people in Britain. However, radio still has plenty of listeners. It has some advantages over television. Transistors can be carried around and used anywhere. Listening to the radio allows people to do other things at the same time, for example cooking, gardening and driving.

For many people, radio is a better medium than television for listening to music, where pictures can be distracting. The same can be said for poetry. Radio drama is an art form in its own right, in which sound is the only means of distinguishing between characters, creating moods and indicating where the action is taking place. Some people prefer radio to television drama,

because they can create their own pictures using their imagination. Here are some views about this:

> 'Listening in the dark prevents attention being distracted ... and the result is that scenes ... can be built up, and characters pictured with amazing vividness.'

> 'I like wireless more than television—the pictures are so much better.'   (*Those Radio Times*)

Listeners have to use their imaginations for radio more than for television and this is why people often call television a less demanding medium than radio.

---

5. **Make a chart, divided into columns headed Television and Radio. List as many different advantages of the two media as you can think of. Think about general advantages and about specific kinds of programmes, e.g. is television or radio better for science or nature programmes? Why? You could illustrate your chart with some simple line drawings.**

---

6. **Imagine you have been asked to write a television and a radio play. Either (a) think up two different ideas, describe them and explain why each is suited to its particular medium; or (b) choose one idea for both media and explain how your treatment of it would be different on radio and on television.**

Chapter 14   The Cinema

The history of the cinema can be traced back to the magic lantern. 'Magic' is a word that goes well with cinema. It has always seemed to be a world of glamour, whose 'stars' seem larger than life, richer and more beautiful than the rest of us. Indeed, the main role of the cinema has been to provide entertainment, rather than to educate, inform or provide news. Of course, there are films that aim to educate, to deal with reality, or to carry a message. And even the most entertaining of films can, through its story, put forward a particular point of view or influence the way we see the world. *Star Wars*, for example, was about a battle between the forces of good and evil. Its message was that good can win.

A magic lantern show, 1858. A picture painted on glass would be slotted into the lantern between a lit candle and the lens. This 'projected' or threw the picture on to a wall or screen.

---

1. **In what way is the main function of the cinema different to that of newspapers, books, radio and television?**

Magic lanterns

The cinema as we know it really began about 80 years ago, but it started with magic lanterns. These were a very simple version of the modern cinema projector. Magic lanterns were enjoyed in Europe over 300 years ago. Often, they were toured from village to village by travelling show people. Wealthier families had shows at home. Magic lanterns were at their most popular in the nineteenth century.

> 'When I was four or five years old, we were taken to a lecture . . . for the sake, no doubt, of the pretty shows we were to see . . . a fine sort of magic-lantern. I did not like the darkness, to begin with; and when Minerva appeared, in a red dress, at first extremely small, and then approaching, till [she] seemed coming directly upon me, it was so like my nightmare dreams that I shrieked aloud.'
>
> (Harriet Martineau, *Autobiography*, 1877)

---

2. **The author is writing about a magic lantern show in 1807. Do you think that the pictures would seem so real and vivid to a child today, who is used to television? Give reasons for your answer.**

The movies

For years, people experimented with ways of showing moving pictures. One method was to show a lot of drawings one after another, so quickly that they gave an impression of movement. This technique is still used in animated cartoons. In 1837, Louis Daguerre invented photography. By 1878 an Englishman called Eadweard Muybridge had successfully photographed movement. He set up a row of cameras and took a series of photographs of a horse running past. When he projected them, it looked as though the horse was actually moving. Music hall owners began to attract audiences by projecting simple moving pictures onto a big screen. Some of the subjects seem rather boring, for example, the arrival of a train or men playing cards, but in those days people were so excited by moving pictures that they didn't much mind what they saw as long as it moved!

By the end of the nineteenth century, cinemas were being built in towns all over Europe and America. Travelling showmen took the cinema into rural communities, too, particularly in England. These 'electric theatres' continued to wander the countryside until the beginning of World War One in 1914. They brought city life and news of the outside world to country people. Even in towns, most audiences were made up of ordinary working people. The cinema widened their horizons. It showed them events, people and places which they could otherwise never have hoped to see. In this sense, the early cinema did have an educational role.

A programme for a film show in 1899.

3. **In what way did the cinema help to educate working people?**

Around 1900, directors began using actors to recreate the news, in films such as *Scenes from the Boer War.* They also made short fiction films. The actors mimed the story. Their words were written underneath or shown in between the pictures. A sound machine or a pianist played music that suited the action on the screen: sad, romantic, military or exciting. The stories were usually about the same kind of people as the audience: ordinary working people. They usually put across Victorian ideas of what was good and bad behaviour, showing that wickedness was punished and virtue rewarded. Bible stories were also popular.

The industry continued to grow. There was a lot of money to be made. This encouraged people to make technical improvements. Silent films were a perfect medium for comedy and great stars like Charlie Chaplin made their names. Adventure stories were also popular. They were often filmed in serials, to bring the audience back each week for the next episode.

Charlie Chaplin.

4. **Why do you think comedy worked so well in silent films?**

5. **What sort of messages did the early silent films offer their audiences?**

Films and the war

The outbreak of World War One in 1914 stopped film-making and cinema-going in Europe. Hollywood, in America, became the centre of world cinema. The content and technique of films got much better. Then, in 1917, America entered the war. There was a flood of films full of battles and heroes and propaganda against Germany.

6. **Why do you think America released so many war films after 1917?**

7. **What sort of messages might these films have carried?**

The war caused terrible suffering and loss of life. After it ended in 1918, the mood of the public in Europe and America was different. The world was a sadder place. Films concentrated less on working people's problems and concerns and more on providing some escape from them. The object was to entertain rather than to *preach.* Heroes and heroines became wealthier and less ordinary. Glamorous stars like Rudolph Valentino became popular.

Chapter 15 The Talkies

Film-makers had been trying for years to add sound to pictures and in the 1920s they found the answer. The 'talkies' were a huge success. Since the war, the cinema had become many people's favourite amusement. Films were now part of life for rich and poor alike. Talking films won the cinema even more fans. In England, hundreds of elaborately decorated cinemas were built, with grand names like the Alhambra and the Majestic. By 1939, over half the population went to the cinema once a week and a quarter went twice a week. Comedies, romances, westerns, gangster films and cartoons poured out of Hollywood during the 1920s and 1930s. During the First World War newsreels became an important part of cinema programmes as well. A few other countries had growing film industries of their own at this time, especially India and Japan.

---

1. **Cinema newsreels became less common after television was introduced. Why do you think this happened?**

Escaping the Depression

In 1929, there was a financial crisis in Europe and America. Businesses went bankrupt. Money and jobs were scarce. There was the possibility of another war. Once again, films reflected the mood of the people. This time they wanted to escape from the unpleasant reality of the Depression and to see films with excitement and glamour. The

Al Jolson, the star of The Jazz Singer, *1926. It was the first full-length talking picture.*

British film industry became more successful. It started producing pictures like *The Life and Times of Henry VIII*. It was full of feasts and merry-making and was seen by over 50 million people.

---

2. **During the Depression escapist films were very popular. What were people escaping from at this time? What did they want from a cinema visit?**

Realism and propaganda

The Second World War broke out in 1939. The British produced films to encourage people in the fight against Germany. In particular, they made *documentaries*. These showed the hard work and heroism of ordinary people such as factory workers, firefighters, ambulance drivers, housewives and the Land Army. These were propaganda films, in that they carried a particular message but they were very well made. Using films as war propaganda was common. In 1942, German films reached over 1000 million people in the numerous countries they had occupied.

---

3. **Why were many British documentaries made about ordinary people during the war?**

---

4. **What sort of feelings did these films aim to encourage?**

After the war, the *realism* of the documentary remained popular. People wanted to see realistic films, which showed life as they knew it. Stories were filmed about the difficulties of everyday life, such as finding a job, and about relationships between ordinary people. Hollywood no longer dominated world cinema. Many European countries built up their own film industries. Cinemagoing was at its most popular.

Cinema visits per year (UK)					
1941	1946	1950	1960	1980	1985
1309 million	1635 million	1396 million	521 million	96 million	70 million

The first real challenge to the film world came with the introduction of television. Television really became popular from 1946, after the war. At first, however, people did not think it was much of a threat to the cinema.

'Film magnates don't have to worry; television will have little effect on films. ... Because in television the most important part of any film is lacking: the audience. A film appeals to several hundred people at the same time; a comedian cracks a joke and there are several hundred laughs; the heroine sheds a tear and several hundred eyes are moist; at the shot of a gun several hundred hearts stop beating. Mass emotion. It is far, far easier to make a crowd of people laugh or cry than to produce the same effect on a solitary person.'

(S. John Woods, *The Radio Times*, 1939)

A scene from Night Shift, *one of many British documentaries made during World War Two about the hard work and bravery of ordinary people.*

5. **Why did John Woods think television would not affect cinema's popularity?**

6. **Can you remember a film that you have seen at which everyone in the audience cried, or jumped out of their seats in fright? Would it have been the same if you had watched it on television? Give reasons for your answer.**

Television, in fact, proved very popular indeed. Cinema audiences dropped dramatically. Many cinemas closed. At the same time, films became much more expensive to make. Producers tried to win back audiences from television with new technology. They introduced Cinerama and Cinemascope, which used much bigger screens, and 3-D and Smell-O-Vision. None were particularly successful. India was one of the few countries where films remained as popular as ever; partly because television was not available to most people there. India still produces more films per year than any other country.

The cinema today

The feelings and problems of the lives of ordinary people are an important subject of modern films, although there is still plenty of demand for adventures, escapism, glamour and excitement. American films remain very popular in Britain, although British films have been more successful recently. More people now watch films at home, on video recorders. This reflects changing social habits in Britain. Ever since the arrival of television, mass entertainment has taken place more in the home and less outside.

7. **Do a survey among your family and friends. Find out how many films they saw in the last two months. Did they watch them in the cinema or at home? If at home, on video or on television? Were the films American, British, European, Australian or other? Make a bar chart like the example below to show your answers, adding them up to make totals.**

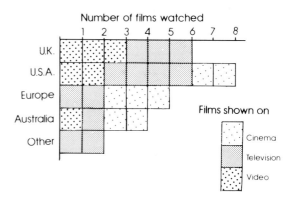

Example:
Me: 4 American (2 TV, 2 cinema), 3 UK (1 video, 2 TV)
Mum: 2 Australian (cinema), 1 European (TV), 1 Indian (TV)
Dad: 2 European (cinema), 1 Australian (video)
John: 4 American (2 video, 2 TV), 2 UK (video)
Susan: 1 European (cinema), 1 Australian (TV)
Mrs Riley: 1 UK (TV), 1 European (TV), 1 African (TV)

8. **Look at the figures for cinema visits. Explain why they have dropped since 1946.**

Chapter 16   Television

Watching television is by far the most popular entertainment in Britain today. Virtually everyone in the country has access to television. Over a third of Britain's households have two or more sets. More than a quarter have video recorders and other equipment, such as home computers. We use these to play games or to tune into television's information systems. Yet only 40 years ago television was a novelty. Very few families owned their own set. And it was only 50 years ago that the world's first regular television service was launched from London's Alexandra Palace.

Shadows and outlines

Scientists had been experimenting with ways of transmitting images for a long time before that dramatic first broadcast in 1936. The first transmission of still pictures took place as far back as 1881. But it was the experiments of John Logie Baird in Britain and C. F. Jenkins in America that made television as we know it possible. In 1925, they successfully transmitted shadows and simple outlines. Four years later, the BBC started to help Baird Television Ltd with their experiments. In 1930, sound was added to the picture. In 1935, a government report recommended setting up a public television service. It was to be paid for by licence fees, like BBC radio.

The historic launch of the world's first regular television service was not seen by many people. There were less than 400 television sets in use. Pictures could be transmitted only within a range of 30 miles. Broadcasting was limited to one hour in the afternoon and one in the evening. Intervals between transmissions were common because of fears about eye strain among 'lookers', as they were called at first.

---

1.   **What factors limited the first television broadcasts?**

Since the nineteenth century, scientists had been predicting the possibility of 'seeing by wireless'. Nevertheless, for most people the idea was beyond their imagination and so the reality was tremendously exciting. Televisions cost at least 60 guineas in 1937 (£1400 in modern money). Since few people could afford sets in the early days,

Dostoevsky's Crime and Punishment, *broadcast in 1953. Television, like radio, was meant to educate rather than just entertain. In the early years, there were many 'serious' discussions, plays and talks.*

owners were encouraged to invite friends in for 'television parties'. Television was only on for a few hours, so families made a point of settling down together for some serious watching.

Self-improvement

John Reith was still director general of the BBC. The stress was on television as a medium for self-improvement and education rather than pure entertainment, just as it had been with radio. In 1939 the BBC's magazine, *The Radio Times*, had a long article about a farm worker who had spent all his savings on a set. He often invited his neighbours in to enjoy his television, which the *The Radio Times* thoroughly approved of. 'He has demonstrated a courage, a spirit of sacrifice, and a desire for self-improvement,' they said. The farmer explained that television gave him a way of 'taking part in the exciting life of London'.

---

2.   **Why do you think that *The Radio Times* gave the farm labourer and his television set so much publicity?**

---

3.   **What reasons did they give for the farm labourer's decision to buy a television?**

---

4.   **What values of television did the article emphasise?**

---

*The thrill of seeing events as they
were actually happening was one of the great
attractions of the new medium.*

*Today television is the most popular way for people to relax.
Britain's electricity supply has to be boosted when the most
popular programmes end because everyone rushes to use their
cookers and kettles!*

History as it happens

As with radio, the feeling of being involved in
great public events while they actually happened
was one of the exciting things about the new
medium for many people. John Reith felt that this
was very important. He believed that the broadcasting media should bring people together in
Britain and the Empire. As people shared the
experience of listening to and watching the important events of their time, he believed they
would gain a far greater sense of being part of
their own history.

Television's first big occasion was the coronation of George VI in 1937. As the BBC Handbook
proudly stated:

> 'When the King and Queen neared Hyde Park Cor-
> ner on their Coronation Coach on May 12, they were
> seen not only by the throng of sightseers lining the
> route, but by an army of people scattered over the
> Home Counties, from Cambridge in the north to
> Brighton in the South.'

At this stage there were only 2000 sets in use
and television's range was limited to the area
around London. It was still the radio that enabled
people throughout Britain and all over the world
to hear the ceremony.

**5. Television and radio gave people the chance
to see and hear important public events, such
as the coronation or the opening of
Parliament. Why did John Reith think this
was important?**

By 1939, there were 20,000 television licence
holders. Before television could become a more
serious rival to radio, however, war was declared.
The government feared that the television transmitter could act as a direction finder for German
bombers. The screens remained blank until June
1946, when they broadcast the Victory Parade.

Television's popularity grew rapidly after the
war. By 1952, over 2 million people owned sets. A
million more sets were purchased before the coronation of Queen Elizabeth II and more than 20
million people watched the coronation. Over $1\frac{1}{2}$
million viewers watched it in Europe. From then
on, more and more families bought their own
television. The urban skyline of Britain changed,
as rooftops everywhere began to sprout aerials.

Chapter 17 Commercial Television

For some time, the government had been considering the idea of another television service besides the BBC. It set up the Independent Television Authority in 1954. This was the start of 'commercial television'. It is called this because the aim of the independent television companies, such as Thames or Yorkshire Television, is to make enough money from selling advertising time to produce their programmes and make a profit for their *shareholders*. The BBC is not a commercial organisation. It is a public corporation, which belongs to the state. There are no shareholders for whom a profit must be made. It gets the money to make its programmes mainly from the sale of television licences, but also from publications and by selling its programmes abroad.

1. **Why was commercial television so called?**

2. **What is the main difference between the way the BBC and commercial television get their money?**

Advertising and the media

The public pay for the BBC by buying licences. They pay for the commercial television by paying the advertising costs, which are built into the price of a product. Advertising and the media are closely linked. Up to half of the space in newspapers and magazines and up to 10 per cent of television time is taken up with advertisements.

Commercial television changed the world of advertising. It brought advertisements right into people's homes. Big business was quick to see the advantages of television. Spending on advertising went right up and television took the largest share.

3. **What did television offer advertisers that other media did not?**

4. **What nineteenth-century example is there of a link between a mass medium and advertising, which led to big changes in that medium?**

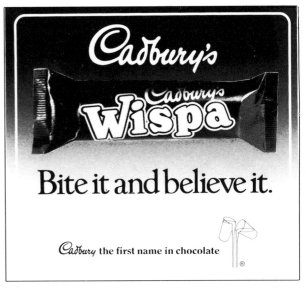

A television advertisement can reach millions of people. Many companies pay about £15,000 for a 30 second commercial.

Here are some views on advertising:

1) It helps us compare prices and brands.
2) It encourages people to be competitive.
3) It informs us of new products.
4) It adds to the price of goods.
5) It increases competition between firms, which forces them to keep their prices as low as possible.
6) It encourages us to buy things we do not need.

5. **Sort these six statements into two columns, headed 'Good Points' and 'Bad Points'. Can you add any more arguments for or against advertising?**

People have questioned whether the BBC should abolish the licence fee and accept advertising. In 1985, the government set up the Peacock Committee to look at different ways of paying for the BBC. In 1986 it produced the Peacock Report, which advised against advertising on the BBC. It suggested a subscription and pay-as-you-view system.

The first commercial television company, ITV, was launched in London in 1955. Other companies

Criss Cross Quiz was very popular in the late 1950s. When the commercial companies first came on the air they broadcast lots of quiz shows and other entertainments to attract audiences.

serving different regions of Britain soon followed. There had been much argument about commercial television. People were concerned that the advertisements would interfere with their enjoyment of the programmes. In the end, most people found that they quickly got used to the advertisements and were not distracted by them. Here are some comments made at the time in Parliament and in the Press:

'I believe independent television is good because competition raises standards.'

'For the first time there will be a choice ... the living room will be a place of more fun—and enlightenment—than ever before.'

'Independent television came simply to satisfy a small group of people who wanted to make a profit ... with the purpose of bringing into every home high-powered salesmanship so that all day ... they are urging you to spend.'

'[Commercial television] is a great danger to the mental and cultural outlook of the people of Britain.'

'Why should advertisements be holy for *The Times* and sinful for television?'

'Commercial television's ... sole interest is not the provision of good programmes ... but whether or not those programmes will cause the people watching them to buy more of certain ... products.'

6. **Sort these views into two columns headed For and Against commercial television.**

7. **Which of these views do you agree with, and why?**

Advertising and the IBA

Every year the IBA checks more than 10,000 television advertisements and 8,000 radio advertisements. About 80 per cent are passed. The others are returned to the advertisers for changes because they could, for example, mislead or upset people.

	General	Medical	Semi-medical	Financial
10,000 television advertisements checked each year	89%	2%	5%	4%
8,000 radio advertisements checked each year	92%	1%	3%	4%

The battle for audiences

Competition for the largest share of the audience soon became fierce. BBC programmes still tended to reflect the view that its role was first to teach and inform, then to entertain. The aim was to give the public 'something slightly better than they think they like' because, as Lord Reith put it, 'few ... know what they want and fewer ... still what they need'. This worthy, if slightly stern, attitude to broadcasting tends to see viewers and listeners as a lot of rather undisciplined children who need to be told what is good for them. It continued for many years. The commercial companies took a rather different approach from 'Aunty Beeb'. They knew they had to win large audiences if they were to be successful. They offered lots of comedies, westerns, crime series and pop shows. By the early 1960s, they claimed that over half of Britain's TV viewers watched them rather than the BBC.

8. **In what ways did commercial television's early programmes differ from those of the BBC?**

9. **Which of the three functions of the media did commercial television concentrate on: entertainment; information; education?**

Chapter 18   The Way Ahead

Commercial television had been successful at winning audiences. However, in 1964 a government report criticised the low standards of television programmes, especially those on ITV. In that same year the BBC launched its second channel, BBC 2. This was more for *minority* interests, in other words those of a small part of the mass audience. It shows, for example, foreign films and science and arts programmes.

This gave the BBC more space on BBC 1 for the 'popular' programmes enjoyed by the majority of the mass audience. As the BBC showed more sports and children's programmes, soap operas, panel games and variety shows, it began to win back its audience from ITV. ITV itself also began to offer more serious programmes. Gradually the difference grew less between the kind of programmes the two companies offered.

---

1. **Why did both the BBC and ITV make some changes in their programmes in the 1960s?**

2. **How did the BBC win back audiences from independent television?**

3. **How do BBC 2 and Channel 4 differ from BBC 1 and ITV?**

BBC 2 and Channel 4 provide programmes, such as Channel 4's Indian film season, which generally attract minority audiences.

In 1967, the BBC introduced Europe's first regular colour transmissions. Two years later, both BBC 1 and ITV were broadcasting in colour. In 1982, the IBA launched Britain's fourth television channel: Channel 4. Like BBC 1 and BBC 2, Channel 4's audiences are smaller because it shows programmes made for minority interests and needs.

In 1983, both the BBC and IBA launched breakfast television, which was already popular in America. Many people felt the British public would not like breakfast television, as most households relied on their radios for the first news of the day. The ITV service, in particular, got off to a slow start. Now both it and the BBC's service seem here to stay. Continuous daytime television started at the end of 1986.

The development of video recorders has had a big impact on our use of television. It gives people the chance to see all the programmes they want to, whenever they choose. Yet researchers have found that many television programmes recorded are never actually watched. Nobody—however keen—can spend all their time watching television! Using video recorders may simply mean that people choose what they watch more carefully.

The information revolution

There have been some dramatic developments in television technology since 1970. One major advance was the introduction of the electronic information services Oracle (ITV) and Ceefax (BBC). These provide pages of news, information and entertainment on the television screen, rather like a televised newspaper or magazine. They cover a wide range of subjects. Computers continually update the information, so that you can be sure of reading the latest financial figures, sports results or weather forecast. Each day, over 1000 changes are made to the news, sports and business sections. Another electronic information service is called Viewdata. In this system, you can communicate with the central computer. To do this, you have to have a two-way cable system or telephone link.

---

4. **What are the advantages and disadvantages of electronic information systems, compared to printed ones such as books or newspapers?**

Americans have a far greater choice of television channels than the British. Cable television has been popular for several years there and until recently it has only operated on a small scale in Britain. The thin cable wires can carry enormous amounts of information. As well as the ordinary national channels they are able to transmit all sorts of special interest channels. For example, you could watch a channel specially for gardeners or dog lovers, or tune into your own community channel, covering local events and issues. With a two-way link you could take part in discussions,

In the near future we will be able to choose from a far wider range of entertainment and information programmes. These will be broadcast to our TV screens and home computers from cables under ground and from satellites in space.

quiz shows and computer games, or go 'teleshopping' or 'telebanking'.

---

6. **Why do you think this kind of television system is called 'narrowcasting' rather than broadcasting?**

7. **Imagine you are a member of a committee setting up a cable television channel for your community. Make a list of the kind of programmes you feel that it should broadcast.**

Television engineers are researching improved picture and sound quality using digital techniques. They are also exploring the potential of direct broadcasting from satellites (DBS). Usually, television stations beam their signals out to space and down to another part of the earth via a satellite. The receiving station then broadcasts the programme to its viewers. With DBS, the viewer can receive signals from all over the world directly. Home satellite receivers are already available in Britain, although only about one person in a million owns one. Numbers are expected to grow fast.

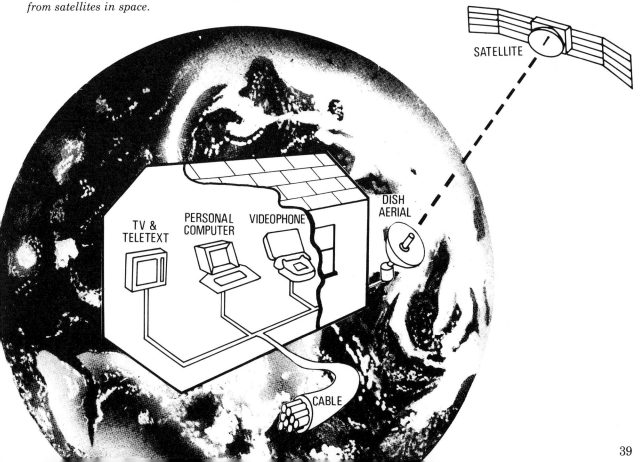

Chapter 19 Television and Society

The history of the media shows how, one by one, inventions and discoveries were made and the modern mass media developed. As soon as a new device became efficient and affordable, it became available to the majority of people and started affecting their lives. Television is the most recent invention yet many people feel that it has affected society more than any other electronic mass medium. It has certainly made the home the centre of people's entertainment.

Television and violence

A constant criticism of television is that the programmes are full of violence—in police thrillers, westerns, war and adventure films and plays. Even the news is full of pictures of fighting, riots and war. Many people feel that Britain is becoming a more violent society. Some blame television for this, although there is no proof of a connection. Here are some of their arguments:

1) People want to copy the violence that they see on television.
2) If people see so much violence in the media, they think that it is the normal way of life and do not try non-violent solutions.
3) Television makes violence and violent people glamorous.
4) It shows unrealistic violence, such as exciting shoot-outs or dramatic car crashes, and ignores the real pain and horror which result, such as people maimed for life, terrified children, or the death of someone you love.
5) People are seen to get away with violence in many programmes.

Some people say that the violence on television helps society, because people can get rid of their feelings of tension and anger simply by watching other people fight and hit each other. It is a way of getting rid of such feelings harmlessly, in the same way as spectators do at a boxing or wrestling match.

Others argue that television is a mirror of our society. Just as a mirror reflects whatever is in front of it, programmes merely reflect the violence that goes on in real life. They claim that there was

'I've told you not to watch that programme! Don't you know it can make you violent?'

A cartoon about violence on television. What point is it making?

the same amount of violence in the past, it was just that people did not know about it.

Before you answer the next question, think about the following information: recent figures show that the average viewer spends the equivalent of nearly seven weeks a year watching television. That is three hours a day. Most children watch for at least two hours a day, which equals one-third of the time they spend at school.

There is one more point to think about. All the media have been criticised not only for producing violent material but also for concentrating on news stories about violence. The *sensational* reporting of crime in the media scares people. Police figures show that people believe that violence is more common than it really is. This can make people mistrustful and suspicious of neighbours and strangers and thus make our society less friendly.

---

1. **Do you think that television**
   (a) encourages violence
   (b) mirrors real life or
   (c) acts as a safety valve?
   Take these three points of view and write down some arguments for each one. Which one do you agree with?

The A Team *is watched by young children. It contains many fights, explosions and gun battles.*

The medium is the message

We've looked at how the messages television puts across may affect people. In 1967 a Canadian writer, Marshall McLuhan, wrote a book called *The Medium is the Message*. He said that it was not so much the programmes we see—the messages that television brings us—that have affected society but the medium of television itself. He argued that it is television viewing, not its content, that has changed social habits and behaviour. It has changed the way we expect to receive information and entertainment. It feeds us with lots of impressions, images and information at great speed. The print media encourage us to reread bits we like or statements we do not understand. The more time and effort we put in, the more we can get out of the print media. But from television we expect lots of action and constantly changing content. It makes fewer demands on our imagination and concentration.

Some teachers feel that this has made children less interested in learning at school. Here is one teacher's point of view:

'Television has accustomed [children] to the highest levels of presentation, to constant *stimulus*, to concentration *spans* of about 30 seconds. ... You can spend a couple of hours preparing a scientific experiment, making sure that everything is alright, [but] unless you reach the standards of what they see on television—programmes that take a week or more to prepare—they feel you are no good. Their attitude is that their video has something better.'

2. **Put into your own words what this teacher is saying.**

3. **In a few sentences, explain why you agree or disagree with the teacher's statement.**

Here are some views on television to think about:

1) Television educates us by bringing us pictures and information about people and events from all over the world.
2) People were happier in the days before mass media because they were not so aware of world's problems.
3) Television brings knowledge of subjects such as nature study, history and science to ordinary people.
4) Television is a thief of time; you can't do anything else while you are watching it.
5) Television keeps the family together because people stay at home to watch it.
6) Television discourages conversation: families 'watch the box' and don't talk to each other any more.
7) Television stimulates conversation and thought.
8) Television requires very little effort from the viewer and so encourages lazy thinking.

4. **Draw two columns headed 'Good Effects' and 'Bad Effects'. Rewrite these sentences, in your own words, in the correct column. Add some more of your own.**

5. **Take two opposing views (such as 7 and 8) and write a few sentences about which one you agree with, and why.**

In the 1960s and 70s, television brought the horror of the Vietnam war into people's homes. Some feel this made people more determined to stop the fighting. Others say that people saw so much violence that after a while they stopped caring.

Chapter 20   The Media and News

1

This shows how news of the 1985 football stadium disaster in Brussels reached the public. Television and radio first broadcast the news (1). The next morning, newspapers carried more pictures, information and interviews (2). Later, the Sunday papers asked "Why did it happen?" and looked in more detail at the causes of football hooliganism (3).

2

3

Each time a new medium has been developed, the existing media have faced the challenge of keeping their audiences. Newspapers were anxious about the arrival of radio. Radio and the cinema were threatened by the invention of television. On the whole, the existing media have always survived the competition, even though there may have been changes in use and popularity. One reason is that each medium has different uses and advantages.

One thing that newspapers, radio and TV have in common is that an important part of their role is to supply the public with news. Yet if we look at the different ways that they communicate news it shows us how they *complement* each other as well as compete with each other. This is important to understanding how and why they have survived. They each give the public a slightly different service. Some of the differences are shown in the chart opposite.

News as entertainment

Here are some more differences to think about. Radio and television offer news broadcasts as part of their overall service. The prime purpose of newspapers, however, is to give the news. And they need to attract readers by the way they do this. They have to 'sell' the news. There can be a danger that the distinction between news and entertainment becomes blurred. For example, an editor may give a story a lot of importance because it will entertain readers and therefore sell copies, not because it really is important news.

What is news? Here are some views:

'News is what someone, somewhere, doesn't want printed. All the rest is publicity.'

'Comment is free but facts are sacred.'

'News is what journalists decide is news.'

'News is what is new, true and interesting.'

'Dog bites man; that's nothing. Man bites dog; that's news.'

'News is what the public is ready and anxious to read.'

'No news is good news.'

1. **Explain in your own words what each statement means.**

2. **Do you agree with any of these statements? Explain why.**

3. **Add your own definition of news to the list.**

4. Look at the chart below and make a list of the main features of each medium, under the headings 'Advantages' and 'Disadvantages'. Add any others you can think of.

Radio	Television	Newspapers
First with the news. Can react instantly to events. Can broadcast information and views from experts and people 'on the spot' quickly.	Can react fast (although slower than radio).	Not as quick or as up to date as TV or radio because each edition is printed some hours before it goes on sale.
No visual image to help understanding.	Supplies photographs, film, maps and diagrams which help our understanding.	Provides photographs, maps, graphics, etc. but only 'stills'.
Listener cannot go back over anything he or she misheard or did not understand.	Viewer cannot go back over any item he or she did not understand.	Can be reread and kept for reference.
News broadcast at close (e.g. hourly) intervals, regularly updated.	News bulletins not as frequent as radio but usually longer and more detailed.	The most regular newspaper is produced only once a day, some are once or twice weekly.
As well as 'hard' news, can provide comment, analysis and background information.	Provides expert and 'on the spot' interviews and current affairs programmes, and documentaries. Sometimes simplifies and shortens the news to fit into programme time.	Gives background information, opinion, analysis and comment, particularly the Sunday papers. Provides much more detail than radio or television. More space than television for interesting but less important items.
Provides local as well as national and international news.	Provides regional but not local news.	Provides local as well as national and international news.
Can broadcast over long distances (e.g. from one country to another).	Long-distance broadcasting requires use of a satellite.	Distribution usually confined to one country or region. Delivery outside this area takes time.
Allows people to do other things while listening, e.g. cook, drive.	Television reporting is more disruptive than newspaper or radio journalism (there are usually several people with lights, cameras and sound machinery, plus a director and other creative staff).	More choice. Readers can pick out items that interest them. They can choose the kind of paper they want to read.

The visual image

One advantage that cinema newsreels, television and newspapers have over radio is the picture. From the mid-nineteenth century, news photographs became more and more common. Pictures can have a powerful effect on the way we view events. In the 1960s and 1970s, the media coverage of America's war in Vietnam deeply affected Americans, many of whom joined in protests against the war. Their newspapers and television channels were full of pictures of the war. Americans could see the suffering and misery, sometimes almost as it happened, even though it was thousands of miles away. One picture of a badly burnt little Vietnamese girl running away from her bombed village (see page 41) became famous as an image that summed up the horror of war for many people. It was an example of the saying, 'one picture is worth a thousand words'.

5. Explain in your own words the meaning of 'one picture is worth a thousand words'.

6. How did the invention of photography change the way the media could report the news?

7. In the early nineteenth century, war was still often thought of as a 'glorious' activity. How might photographs have changed the way that ordinary people saw war?

A recent example of the power of the image is the effect that one short television film of the famine in Ethiopia had. It stirred the British public to raise huge sums of money to help. Articles had been written about the famine for months but it took pictures of the suffering to move people to action.

Chapter 21   The Media Worldwide

The fight against the 'tax on knowledge' in Britain in the eighteenth and nineteenth centuries showed how strongly people believed in the right of everyone to have access to news about the world they live in. By this they did not mean only that the working family, however poor, should be able to afford a newspaper. They also meant that newspapers should contain news and information about the things which mattered to ordinary working people. In other words, news should be written for them and about them.

Good news is no news?

This same idea is behind a criticism which many Third World countries have about the media. Generally speaking, the countries of the Third World are in the southern part of the globe, making up most of Asia, Africa and South America. They feel that most of the news distributed around the world is written for and about the 'rich', industrialised nations, which are largely in the north. In particular, they feel the countries of the 'North' tend to ignore any good news about the poorer 'South'. The media prefer to report disasters, which make dramatic stories. The general public is always hearing about droughts, floods, civil war and famine in these countries. Economic or scientific progress or cultural events are rarely reported. Such stories do not sell papers, nor make exciting television programmes. The Third World feels that the flow of information worldwide therefore gives a distorted picture of what goes on outside the rich world. For example, people in Europe and North America hear a lot about famine and fighting in Africa—but little about its music, art and theatre or its business and scientific success stories.

---

1. **Why do people in the Third World complain about the way that events in their countries are reported by the media?**

Part of the reason for this imbalance is historical. The main international news agencies were set up by the richer countries, some in the nineteenth century. Their main customers are still rich countries, so they report the sort of news that

Bob Geldof used the media of radio and TV to broadcast a pop concert worldwide. It raised huge sums of money to help famine victims in Ethiopia.

these nations want to know about. In addition, the information that the agencies gather worldwide goes through their main offices, in America or Europe. There it is edited and sent out worldwide again. This means that newspaper offices in, for example, neighbouring African countries may find that they receive news about each other via London or New York. That is a little like being a British journalist and finding that the only information your newspaper could get about America has been written by the Chinese.

The western agencies said that the content of news they put out was not *biased* against the South. However, in 1983 it was estimated that less than a quarter of their news output was about the Third World—where three-quarters of the world's population live.

The South wanted the North to help them with the expensive task of setting up another international agency, which would enable their news and their voices to be heard as loudly as those of richer countries. It would distribute news written for the Third World by the Third World. This is how Indira Gandhi, then the prime minister of India, described the need for such an agency: 'We want to hear Africans on events in Africa. You should similarly be able to get an Indian explanation of events in India.'

---

2. **Explain why Mrs Gandhi supported the idea of a Third World news agency.**

Rescue workers look for survivors of the Mexico earthquake. Media coverage of the disaster moved people in other countries to send help.

In 1976, 85 Third World countries got together to create their own agency. Some of the developed countries were worried about this, because some of the countries in the agency do not have a free press. Their press and broadcasting services are run by their governments. Thus the agency could become a means of sending out government propaganda and some news could be more biased than anything the western agencies send out. In spite of these difficulties, the idea has been accepted that there should be more news about the Third World—and more news flowing directly between Third World countries.

A force for good?

The media's interest in disasters can do good. A television film about starving Ethiopians brought home to Britain the horror of something happening millions of miles away. Bob Geldof then used the media of radio and television to broadcast a pop concert all over the world and raise millions of pounds. The media can mislead people, however, by giving an incomplete picture. The media stressed the suffering in Ethiopia because they wanted to raise money. They did not show the way that many Ethiopians are proudly and quietly helping each other. Also, Ethiopia is not Africa, any more than Spain is Europe. Africa is a continent, like Europe, and is made up of many different peoples and countries, with quite different customs and traditions, advantages and problems, landscapes and resources. Media attention on Ethiopia has saved lives. But it does need to be balanced by more positive information, to increase people's understanding and knowledge of Ethiopia, and of Africa as a whole.

---

3. **'A little knowledge is a dangerous thing'. Do you think that this proverb applies to the way that people receive information through the mass media?**

---

4. **Use these words in a sentence to show that you understand their meaning: bias, propaganda.**

---

5. **Study this picture carefully. Notice the expensive camera equipment. Why do you think the photographer took this picture? Write a few sentences about the questions this image raises.**

Journalists photograph a famine victim.
The Western press has been criticised for concentrating on poverty, hunger and conflict in the Third World.

Chapter 22 Living with the Mass Media

In the past, some people with political, religious or financial power tried to control the spread of the print medium. Today, the print and broadcasting mass media reach larger audiences than those people ever dreamt possible. Even a 'minority interest' television programme reaches a million people or more. Politicians, in particular, soon began to recognise the power of the media to win them votes. One hundred years ago, someone making a speech would not have been able to reach anything like the number of people possible today with radio or television.

However, there are some disadvantages to communication with mass television or radio audiences. A speaker addressing people at a meeting can be booed, cheered, heckled, questioned or applauded. They can see the effect that their words are having. The television or radio speaker has no idea how his or her audience is responding. The speech may be winning them over, putting them off, infuriating them or simply boring them. But since the speaker is talking at them, and not with them, he or she can't tell. Communication via the mass media is less of a two-way process. It is a *monologue*, not a *dialogue*.

1. **Look up 'monologue' and 'dialogue' in the glossary. What is the difference between them?**

2. **Why is communication by television or radio less of a two-way process than making a speech to a crowd?**

The media and politics

Stanley Baldwin, prime minister of Britain in the 1930s, was one of the first politicians to realise the importance of using the media. In the 1935 election, he had a great advantage over his political rivals as he was very skilled at coming across well on radio, which was the mass media of his time. Baldwin realised that radio needed a different style of speaking. Here is how one journalist described his success:

'He alone talked; the others *orated*. They wrote out speeches and delivered them in a platform tone. From a platform, they would have sounded well. The audience would have *collaborated*. Cheers and laughter and interruptions would have helped the speakers out. Without such aid, they sounded ... thin and dry. Mr Baldwin's ... effort came near to being a chat, while the rest were—just speeches'.

(*The Radio Times*, 1937)

3. **Explain in your own words how Baldwin used radio more successfully than his political rivals.**

Today, the media play an important part in political elections all over the world. In the 1985 elections in India, politicians used television, film and radio to get their messages across. They persuaded famous film stars to support their campaigns. Several film stars actually stood for Parliament. Their tremendous popularity won them many votes.

The President of the United States, Ronald Reagan, is a former film actor. His skill in front of the cameras was a vital part of his successful campaign. His rival, Jimmy Carter, was said to have a 'poor media image'. He seemed to be weaker and less sure of himself. Politicians who are good 'media personalities' have a great advantage over those who appear to be dull, uncertain or incompetent, even though they may not actually be any of these things. It is hardly surprising that major politicians today hire advisers to help them with their 'media image'.

Roy Jenkins faces the press. Today, politicians who are good 'media personalities' have an advantage over those who are not.

Political parties all over the world now use media stars to help win votes. Amitabh Bachchan (right) is a popular film actor who won a seat in the Indian Parliament in 1985.

In addition, the British public today do have access to more information about what is going on in the world. There is more debate about how the country is run. It would be harder for a government to cover up wrongdoings now than in previous centuries. The Press can act like a 'public watchdog' and investigate and report on injustices. They can act as a voice for people who feel that they are being treated unfairly.

People's knowledge of the world is wider, too. Through the mass media, the British public learn about the problems other countries and societies are having and of their different ways of solving them. Nature and other programmes show people the world's varied natural resources and cultures. The new communications technology, such as cable television, will bring an even wider range of information and opinion.

Thirty years ago, an MP named Clement Davis made this statement in Parliament:

> '[Television] is the most likely of all discoveries made in this amazing age to have the greatest influence upon mankind, for it brings us all, from all the countries of the world, into close and intimate knowledge of one another and of our ideas and thoughts'. (*Hansard*, 1953)

4. **Explain briefly how the relationship between the media and politicians has changed during this century.**

5. **What might be the dangers of electing a politician because he or she comes across well on television?**

6. **Marshall McLuhan said that the important point about the mass media is not so much its content but the way it has influenced society. In what way has the media affected modern politics?**

7. **Do you agree or disagree with this statement? Give your reasons.**

The mass media have given us far wider knowledge of the world's cultures and societies than previous generations. For example, the TV series The Heart of the Dragon *explored Chinese history and civilisation.*

A question of choice

We have looked at some of the different opinions that people have about the mass media. There is plenty of argument about their values and advantages. Perhaps the one thing on which there is agreement is that they have played an important part in Britain's social and economic history and that they continue to affect our lives in many different ways. Not all of these may be to everyone's benefit but few would disagree that much of the material we can now choose to read, watch or listen to is excellent. There is plenty of low quality material, too. The choice is ours.

THE ELECTRONIC MEDIA:

1792	First telegraphic device invented
1837	First patent granted for electric telegraph
	Louis Daguerre invents photography
1866	Telegraph cable laid between UK and USA
1881	First transmission of still pictures
1899	Marconi sends wireless message from UK to France
1914	Silent films widespread
1922	British Broadcasting Company (radio) formed
1927	British Broadcasting Company becomes British Broadcasting Corporation
	First full-length talking film released
1936	BBC Television starts broadcasting
1946	Cinema-going at its most popular: 1635 million visits a year
1954	Independent Television Authority (ITA) set up
1955	London ITV service opens (other regional companies open over the following 8 years)
1961	First communications satellite, Telstar, in orbit
1964	BBC 2 launched
1967	BBC's first local radio station launched
	Colour introduced on BBC 2
1969	Colour introduced on BBC 1 and ITV
1972	ITA assumes responsibility for Independent Local Radio (ILR) and becomes the IBA (Independent Broadcasting Authority)
1973	First ILR service opens (LBC)
1981	Seven cable TV systems start experimental operations
1982	Channel 4 launched
1983	BBC 1 and ITV launch breakfast-time services
1986	Peacock Committee Report

THE PRINT MEDIA:

800s	Chinese develop block printing
1100s	Arabs bring art of papermaking to Europe
1455	Johann Gutenberg invents movable type
1476	William Caxton prints first English book
1702	*The Daily Courant*, first English daily newspaper, published
1709	Copyright Act passed
1712	Penny tax on every sheet of newspaper imposed
1772	Press allowed to report Parliamentary debates
1785	First issue of *The Times*
1815	Newspaper tax raised to fourpence a sheet
1853	Newspaper Advertisement Tax abolished
1855	Newspaper Stamp Tax abolished
1861	Newsprint Tax removed
1896	*Daily Mail*, the first 'popular' paper, launched
1919	Public Libraries Act
1935	First Penguin paperback published
1986	*Today*, first newspaper to use computer colour technology, launched

WORDS IN TEXT:

access   the means to reach/have something
bias   favouring one direction or opinion
bribe   money offered to someone to do something
bulletin   an announcement of news
circulation   average sales of a newspaper or magazine
complement   to add to, or to complete something
copyright   the right to use written work or music
culture   various kinds of learning, music, art, etc
debate   a discussion or public argument
dialogue   a talk between two or more people
documentary   a film showing people in real life
edit   to prepare something for printing or broadcasting
escapism   avoiding real life
highbrow   intellectual, 'brainy'
fiction   something imagined or made up
function   job, role, work
leisure   spare time
libel   statement which damages a person's character
minority   the smaller part
monologue   a speech or talk by one person
pamphlet   booklet, usually dealing with an issue of the time
patron   one who protects or supports another
popularise   to make something appeal to the majority of people
preach   to put across religious or moral ideas
propaganda   spreading ideas and information to make people believe something
realism   dealing with the facts of real life
sensational   very exciting
serial   story told in several episodes
shareholders   people who own shares in a business
subscription   a regular payment
technology   the science of tools and how things work
territorial   area belonging to a nation
transmit   to send out radio or television programmes
transportation   sent away from Britain, usually to Australia

WORDS IN QUOTATIONS:

appointed   equipped
collaborate   join in
complacent   self-satisfied
cone   circular object
culpable   guilty
democracy   government by the people
enmity   hatred
foresight   thinking ahead
incurred   brought upon himself
orate   to give a speech
remnant   remains
repose   relaxation
solitary   single
span   length
stimulus   excitement
unprejudiced   without an already fixed opinion